THE TROPHY KIDS GROW UP

how the **millennial generation** is shaking up the workplace

Ron Alsop

JOSSEY-BASS
A Wiley Imprint
www.josseybass.com

THE WALL STREET JOURNAL.

Published by Jossey-Bass
A Wiley Imprint
989 Market Street, San Francisco, CA 94103-1741—www.josseybass.com

Jossey-Bass books and products are available through most bookstores. To contact Jossey-Bass directly call our Customer Care Department within the U.S. at 800-956-7739, outside the U.S. at 317-572-3986, or fax 317-572-4002.

Jossey-Bass also publishes its books in a variety of electronic formats. Some content that appears in print may not be available in electronic books.

Library of Congress Cataloging-in-Publication Data
Alsop, Ronald.
    The trophy kids grow up : how the millennial generation is shaking up the workplace / Ron Alsop.
        p. cm.
    Includes index.
    ISBN 978-0-470-22954-5 (cloth)
    1. Generation Y—Employment. 2. Generation Y—Attitudes. 3. Organizational behavior. 4. Intergenerational relations. 5. Work ethic.
    I. Title. II. Title: Millennial generation is shaking up the workplace.
    HD6270.A44 2008
    331.3'40973—dc22
                                                                2008029696

Printed in the United States of America
FIRST EDITION
HB Printing   10 9 8 7 6 5 4 3 2 1

Contents

To Matthew, my millennial generation son

Preface

"Here come the millennials—the next big wave of M.B.A. students."

That was the opening sentence of a column I wrote in 2006 for *The Wall Street Journal* about business schools bracing for the imminent arrival of the millennial generation. It wasn't long before I realized that I had really touched a nerve. As soon as the article appeared in print and online, the e-mails and phone calls began, and they didn't stop for days. I heard from millennials, their parents, corporate recruiters and managers, even retirees who didn't like the sound of these confident, demanding youngsters. Many people agreed with the points in my article, but there were a few dissenters who didn't appreciate some of the criticism of millennials. What struck me most, however, was the passion in many of the messages.

A mother in California described her children as "over-achieving, scared, and exhausted" after surviving the brutal college admissions process. "I can attest to the sense that these top students have of never being good enough; what they do have, as far as attitude goes, is resentment," she wrote in her e-mail.

"They are definitely not a humble group having worked so darned hard to get into these top schools."

I realized that there was much more to explore as this generation continues to move into colleges and the workplace. It was clear to me that the millennials will remain of keen interest because of the many notable differences in their expectations, skills, and attitudes.

The result of my journalistic exploration is *The Trophy Kids Grow Up*, a look at how the millennial generation is shaking up colleges and, in particular, the workplace. I interviewed dozens of millennials, parents, professors, college admissions and career services directors, and corporate recruiters and managers, as well as drew information from various surveys of young people and employers.

Generational researchers variously categorize and label the young people born in the 1980s and 1990s as millennials, generation Y, and generation next. The NetGeneration and the iGeneration also are popular monikers because young people are so technology oriented and always connected to an iPod or other digital device. Some researchers and consultants have set different beginning and ending dates for this generation, but most agree on many of its defining traits.

Generation Y remains a popular term, but in this book, I will primarily use *millennials*, a label popularized by the generational experts Neil Howe and William Strauss and one that many young people seem to prefer.

In Chapter One, I provide a portrait of the trophy kids and highlight both their strengths and foibles. Subsequent chapters describe in greater detail the millennial generation's most salient attributes, particularly as they are playing out in the workplace. I also show how companies are changing tactics to recruit millennials in the Internet age, and I take a look at some of this generation's dream jobs.

Because parents are so central to the lives of the millennials, I decided to devote two chapters to their relationships with their children and the "helicopter parent" phenomenon that is rattling colleges and employers. In fact, the title of this book is based on the fact that many proud, protective parents view their accomplished millennial children as their "trophy kids."

In my research, I found the millennials frequently written off as narcissistic, arrogant, and fickle. Although there is certainly some truth in such negative perceptions, the millennials also can be quite impressive in their ambitions and achievements. They are a generation of conflicting characteristics—self-absorbed but also civic minded, for instance. Keep in mind, however, that the traits ascribed to the millennials certainly don't apply to every member of that generation. They are common but not universal attributes.

My own reporting experiences brought home to me some of the millennial generation's tendencies. When I tried to contact a college student via e-mail, for example, there was no response for days. But she replied within minutes when contacted on Facebook. Clearly, e-mail is fine for baby boomers like me, but not for this social networking, instant messaging generation. I also observed the generation's job-hopping behavior firsthand. When I tried to contact a couple of millennials for follow-up questions a few months after the initial interviews, they had already left their employers.

There's still much uncertainty about how the millennials and employers will adapt to one another. Will millennials mature into strong leaders who can give direction rather than depend on others for guidance? Will companies evolve to meet the millennials' demands for work-life balance? And will millennials stay true to their professed desire to help fix some of the world's most pressing problems, from poverty to global warming? Only time will tell, but the millennials clearly represent a new breed of student, worker, and global citizen.

This book focuses on some of the colleges, companies, and other organizations that are taking the lead in understanding and reaching out to the millennials. I spent extensive time with some of the major student recruiters, particularly management consulting, accounting, and investment banking firms. Their experiences in recruiting and managing millennials will provide valuable lessons for other companies about what to expect in their new hires and how they may have to adapt to them. Employers clearly cannot afford to ignore millennials because of the imminent need for talent to replace retiring baby boomers. If companies don't take notice of the striking differences of this generation and prepare to deal with them, they are sure to lose the battle for the best talent.

I also hope that millennials and their parents find the book enlightening. It will help them see how the world perceives this generation and discover which employers are most millennial-friendly. Millennials also will learn that they will probably have to adjust their expectations if they hope to make the most of their talents and realize their personal and professional dreams.

Finally, I thank the many corporate managers and university officials who generously shared their insights; my thanks also go to the millennials and parents whom I interviewed. Their personal stories serve as a mirror on this generation's attitudes and aspirations. I was pleasantly surprised by the openness of the millennials I met; their honesty is truly refreshing in our cynical world.

I also acknowledge Kathe Sweeney, my editor at Jossey-Bass, and Roe D'Angelo, a longtime colleague at *The Wall Street Journal*, who have been enthusiastic supporters of my book. My friend Bruce Brown deserves special thanks for his many insights and his encouragement. And I express my appreciation to my own millennial son, Matthew, an accomplished young man who has high expectations and makes me very proud, and to his mother, Marybeth, who, like me, wants to give him the very best in life but also to avoid becoming an overly protective helicopter parent.

Now, meet the millennials and learn how this remarkable generation promises to stir up the workplace and perhaps the world.

Summit, New Jersey   Ron Alsop
July 2008

1

The Trophy Kids

Larissa Kravanja always believed she could achieve whatever she put her mind to. So far, she hasn't disappointed herself.

The University of Virginia graduate, now in her mid-20s, has been ascending the corporate ladder at Merrill Lynch & Co. and looking forward to eventually attending one of America's top law schools. An admittedly obsessive list maker, Kravanja continually sets new objectives for herself. Soon after her college graduation, she made a list of goals she hoped to reach by age 25, including running two half marathons, taking the entrance exams for graduate school and law school, getting promoted at Merrill Lynch, and moving from Brooklyn to Manhattan. She achieved all of them, but just barely; her move to Manhattan took place less than a month before her 25th birthday in 2008. She also reached a significant milestone not on her list: living with her boyfriend.

Kravanja's to-do list for the next five years is still taking shape, but it already includes starting law school, figuring out her subsequent career plans, embracing a less stressful "day-by-day approach" to life, and learning to cook. "I sometimes get shocked looks from my older colleagues at Merrill when I talk openly about getting ready to go to law school," she says. "They think I must hate what I'm doing now, but that's not the case. I just believe in planning ahead."

Kravanja embodies many of the characteristics of the millennial generation born between 1980 and 2001. Like a quintessential millennial, Kravanja counts both career achievements and community service among her top priorities in life. In fact, she had expected to join a nonprofit organization after college, despite two summer internships at Merrill Lynch as an analyst in the retirement and insurance groups. But she was lured back to Merrill by a full-time job in the multicultural marketing group. She soon was promoted to assistant vice president for global diversity and inclusion, overseeing the brokerage and investment banking firm's "professional network" groups for minorities and women. "Now, my whole day job is giving back to our employees," she says. In addition, she does volunteer work for the organization Upwardly Global, mentoring highly skilled immigrants on job-search strategies.

In the workplace, Kravanja shows her millennial stripes in her desire for a flexible schedule and a casual culture. She usually manages to adjust her work hours for personal needs, but in Merrill Lynch's more formal atmosphere, she must leave her jeans at home and only listen to her iPod as circumstances permit.

Self-confident and impatient, she wishes she could speed up her career progress. "People tell me I need to be more patient, that I will get rewarded in time," she says. "But at times, it's hard to be patient for the bigger reinforcement pay-offs like bonuses and promotions." She also needs regular feedback about how she's doing. "It's very millennial of me, I guess," she says. "I don't need a daily pat on the back, just a big pat when I finish a big project. I probably need it so much because my mom has been giving me feedback since day one."

She keeps in touch with her mother on a near daily basis and still welcomes her guidance. "She hasn't influenced me much about college or Merrill Lynch," Kravanja says. "As I'm growing up and away from her, the advice is more about domestic things like moving to a new apartment. But she still wants to keep up on everything that's happening in my life."

Millennials like Kravanja are truly "trophy kids," the pride and joy of their parents. They and their parents have placed a high premium on success, filling resumes with not only academic accolades but also a smorgasbord of sports and other extracurricular activities, volunteer work in their local communities, and exotic travels abroad. The trophy kids were lavishly praised when they made the grade—and sometimes even when they didn't, to avoid damaging their self-esteem.

Since nursery school, the trophy kids have been prepping to get into the best colleges. James Danko, the business school dean at Villanova University in Pennsylvania, even received an Excel spreadsheet that an applicant's parents had used to record their child's accomplishments through the years. "It's a credentials-driven generation, no doubt about it," Danko says. "I have to give them credit for their drive and ambition, but there's sometimes almost too much intensity in competing with peers. It gets to the point that they feel they need to take college courses in the summer and have double, even triple majors to keep their edge."

Now what happens when these trophy kids, who have always felt special, arrive in the workplace with greater expectations than any generation before them? That's what companies are gradually discovering as they recruit more and more millennials. "This generation of young people is quite serious about reshaping the work environment to conform to their personal goals and lives," says Daphne Atkinson, a consultant on business schools and management education. "Although their every want and expectation won't be met, they will definitely make employers sit up and take notice."

Indeed, employers face some of their biggest management challenges ever as they try to integrate millions of millennials into a workplace with three other very different generations. In addition to the millennials, there are the traditionalists— also referred to as the veteran, mature, or silent generation— born between 1925 and 1945; the baby boomers, 1946 to 1964; and generation Xers, 1965 to 1979. (See the accompanying table for a summary of the characteristics of the four generations in the workplace.) Already, the trophy kids are at odds with some members of the other generations, who perceive them as arrogant and unwilling to adapt to the corporate culture. Their trademark flip-flops and ripped jeans, ubiquitous iPods, and preference for text messages rather than face-to-face communication are driving some older colleagues and managers nuts.

Four Generations in the Workplace

	Millennials	Gen Xers	Baby Boomers	Traditionalists
Time Span	1980–2001	1965–1979	1946–1964	1925–1945
Current U.S. Residents, Census Bureau Estimate	92 million	62 million	78.3 million	38.6 million
Key Historical Events	Columbine High School shootings, September 11 terrorist attacks, Enron and other corporate scandals, wars in Afghanistan and Iraq, Hurricane Katrina	AIDS epidemic, space shuttle Challenger catastrophe, fall of the Berlin Wall, Oklahoma City bombing, Bill Clinton–Monica Lewinsky scandal	Vietnam War, assassinations of John and Robert Kennedy and Martin Luther King Jr., first man on the moon, Kent State killings, Watergate	Great Depression, Pearl Harbor, World War II, Korean War, Cold War era, Cuban missile crisis
Traits	Entitled, optimistic, civic minded, close parental involvement, values work-life balance, impatient, multitasking, team oriented	Self-reliant, adaptable, cynical, distrusts authority, resourceful, entrepreneurial, technology savvy	Workaholic, idealistic, competitive, loyal, materialistic, seeks personal fulfillment, values titles and the corner office	Patriotic, dependable, conformist, respects authority, rigid, socially and financially conservative, solid work ethic

In contrast to the millennials, the traditionalists, many of whom have already retired, respect the status quo and bring a strong sense of loyalty to their jobs. Graying baby boomers, who are on the verge of retirement or at least a switch to part-time status, earned a reputation for being workaholics and consider their careers an integral part of their identity.

Resourceful and self-reliant, generation Xers don't trust institutions and don't expect job security. Together, the four generations make for an intriguing and potentially explosive brew.

It will take more than a decade for yet another generation to join the workforce. Although it's a little early to start characterizing the children born after 2001, some researchers already are concocting generational names. Because the millennials are sometimes referred to as generation Y, generation Z is naturally one of the labels being attached to the next cohort. Largely the offspring of generation X, this up-and-coming group is also being called zeds, gamers, the new millennials, and the homeland generation, a reference to homeland security in this age of terrorism.

For now, though, most of the attention is aimed squarely at the millennials. In some ways, educators and employers have found that they exhibit a number of contradictory attitudes and behaviors. "It's all about me" might seem to be the mantra of these self-absorbed young people who aspire to be financially successful so they can pay off college loans and afford their digital toys, international travels, and other pleasures. But many millennials like Kravanja also demonstrate strong concern about social and environmental issues and tend to be active in community service. In another interesting twist, they want structure and clear direction in their work assignments, but they also expect flexibility to decide when and where they complete the tasks. And although they crave individual praise and recognition, they can also be terrific team players, whether in sports, the classroom, or the workplace.

Millennials also are a polarizing generation. They have many fans who admire their optimism, intelligence, ambition, and commitment to make the world a better place. But they also come in for some stinging criticism for their inflated expectations. Employers, in particular, have mixed feelings about millennials. While respecting their aptitude for technology and their ability to work well in teams, many recruiters and managers find millennials far too demanding when it comes to needing guidance, frequent performance appraisals, rapid career advancement, and work-life balance. Although many of them are well educated, millennials strike employers as being book smart but suffering from a deficit of common sense. How else to explain the job candidate who showed up late for an interview at a public relations agency with chewing gum in her mouth and blue, chipped fingernails?

Some employers even go so far as to call millennials slackers, although they actually can be incredibly efficient, productive workers as long as their job is engaging and will help advance their careers. But if they find work boring and unfulfilling, they'll be out the door in a snap. Such behavior causes bitterness among many employers, who bemoan such disloyalty and the resulting low retention rates.

Whether they like the millennials or not, farsighted companies know they must try to accommodate them because they are America's future workforce as the large baby-boom generation moves into its twilight years. According to U.S. Census Bureau population estimates, America's millennial generation currently numbers about 92 million, compared with 78.3 million baby boomers.

"We have to understand that millennials simply view the world differently from us, and try to adapt to them," says Rich Garcia, director of enterprise recruiting and retention at State

Farm Mutual Automobile Insurance Co. in Bloomington, Illinois. "We can't let ourselves get bogged down in thinking they're not loyal. Instead, we need to give them a voice in the organization and learn to work with them, not against them."

Cam Marston, founder of the consulting firm Generational Insight, has observed heightened interest in understanding the millennials, particularly among technology, health care, consulting, accounting, and other professional services firms that vie aggressively for talent. "With each passing week, it's becoming clearer that this is a very different generation," he says. "More companies are trying to understand those differences and make changes to attract these young people. Some are doing it willingly, others more begrudgingly."

L'Oréal is not only willing but actually quite enthusiastic about welcoming more millennials to its beauty-products business. "The millennial generation is at the top of my agenda of priorities," declares François de Wazières, director of international recruitment for Paris-based L'Oréal. "We're very seriously investing in knowing these people's characteristics and how we can recruit and manage them to the fullest efficiency." To that end, L'Oréal, together with an organization of European business schools, has launched a study of millennials' values and attitudes.

"I believe the millennials will be a gold mine of talent for L'Oréal because they are such a good fit with our emphasis on innovation, creativity, open-mindedness, and entrepreneurial spirit," de Wazières says. "Of course, we will have to explain to middle managers and executives that they will want to wear jeans and T-shirts and have flexibility in their work life. But we will also have to draw a line between what we will accept and what we won't."

Certainly not all the characteristics that demographers, educators, and employers ascribe to millennials apply to each and every member of the generation. There are exceptions to any generalization. In fact, the various millennial traits tend to most closely fit college students and graduates, who are of greatest interest to corporate recruiters. Some of the attributes also could describe generation X, which is known for being technology savvy and seeking work-life balance, too. But even those two qualities resound much more strongly with the millennials. Clearly, the trophy kids are emerging as a quite distinctive and fascinating group of young people who will command the world's attention for many years to come.

A MILLENNIAL PORTRAIT

The millennials are fast on their way to rivaling the baby boomers as the most studied generation. They are sometimes referred to as "echo boomers" because many of them are the offspring of boomers, who have helped shape them and continue to play a major role in their lives. Whether they will affect the world as much as the boomers did remains uncertain, of course, but they are certainly promising to make waves.

The trophy kids have generally enjoyed financial and emotional security in their close, comfortable relationships with their families. But their lives also have been touched by a succession of momentous events, including the Columbine High School shootings; the September 11, 2001, terrorist attacks; the wars in Iraq and Afghanistan; Hurricane Katrina; and the wave of corporate scandals that began with the collapse of Enron Corp.

One of the most avid watchers of millennials has been Northwestern Mutual Life Insurance Co. Between 1997 and

2004, it put millennials under the microscope for five research studies on "America's emerging leaders." Some of the earliest surveys detected an unusually optimistic, self-assured generation. But among the findings in Northwestern Mutual's 2004 survey of 21- to 23-year-olds: heightened anxiety because they're living in a world in conflict. Indeed, the millennials surveyed consider growing up faster and a lack of innocence as two of the chief disadvantages of their generation. They also were pessimistic about America's direction and its leadership, but enthusiastic about their connections to family and friends.

Their dissatisfaction with political leaders obviously has motivated the millennials to action. They were quite active during the 2008 presidential primaries, with more young people voting than in recent years and especially strong support for Barack Obama and his campaign theme of "change we can believe in." In a survey of 18- to 24-year-olds in fall 2007, Harvard University's Institute of Politics found that 41% definitely planned to vote in a 2008 primary or caucus and 61% intended to vote in the general election.

Although the threat of terrorism has shaken the millennials as it has all the generations, young people still tend to have high self-esteem and plenty of hope and ambition. That's certainly the case with Steffen Ringelmann, a graduate of Vassar College who is happily pursuing his artistic passions in New York City. After graduation in 2004, he floated around a bit, waiting tables so he could paint and do volunteer work at a free monthly publication in Brooklyn and an art gallery in Manhattan. Feeling a bit exhausted and overwhelmed, he spent three months chilling out on the coast of Maine, then headed to Berlin, Germany, for four months. Now back in New York City, he works as an assistant at a furniture and design gallery and builds furniture in the evenings and on weekends for a major advertising agency and other customers.

"My goal is to be a tastemaker and have an influence on style," he says. "I have found my path in life in design and can see myself succeeding financially, as well as emotionally and creatively." He agrees that his generation is self-involved and less willing to join the rat race. "I want to explore, deconstruct, and understand my own sense of self through the act of creation," he says. Then he adds, laughing, "It's about me, me, me, me, me!"

Not content to be simply their parents' trophy kids, many millennials dream of riches and world renown. In a 2006 study of 18- to 25-year-olds labeled "generation next," the Pew Research Center in Washington, DC, found that they believe that their generation's top goals in life are being rich and famous. Similarly, in a 2007 Harris Interactive survey, 56% of 13- to 21-year-olds said their dream is to be a millionaire, and about a third aspired to become a famous musician or singer. About 40%, however, envisioned a nobler achievement: curing diseases.

Whether or not stardom is within their reach, this digital generation clearly loves attention and cyberfame. It's a celebrity-obsessed group that grew up on *American Idol*, entertainment tabloids, and Internet gossip. The millennials share the most mundane—and most sensational—aspects of their lives on such social networking sites as Facebook and MySpace, opine in blogs, and post their personal video creations on YouTube. They are so casual and indiscreet that much of their life is an open book online, where they display racy photos, boast about their sexual exploits, and try to rack up the most virtual "friends" or connections. Older adults believe they have no sense of privacy and warn them that their exhibitionism could ultimately hurt their careers and personal lives.

Ringelmann finds MySpace and Facebook "guilty pleasures" and incredibly valuable ways to connect with new people and possibly promote his furniture designs. But he also finds the connections rather shallow. "My generation is very social and gets to know a lot of people online, but we don't have many good friends through our networks," he says. "I think we're a very socially distracted generation because of the Internet."

The avid social networking is but one manifestation of the tremendous influence of technology on the millennials. Always connected to cell phones, iPods, laptops, or video-game players, this generation—sometimes called the MyPod Generation—has mastered multitasking skills better than any other. At the same time, however, educators and employers complain that the informal, shorthand style of text and instant messaging has impaired young people's writing abilities and interpersonal communication skills. What's more, the digital generation's tendency to do multiple things at once may be resulting in shorter attention spans.

Another hallmark of the millennial generation is its prolonged adolescence. Many young people like Ringelmann are drifting awhile, delaying marriage, children, home ownership, and even a steady career until well into their 20s or even their 30s. But they aren't being frivolous Peter Pans; they're just taking longer to explore the possibilities before assuming major responsibilities. They want to control their destinies and are afraid of making choices that could prove to be mistakes. Failure to them, in the end, is never finding their true passion.

Consequently, they tend to be job hoppers, often living at home with their parents, who provide a financial safety net. In a 2005 Pew Research Center survey, nearly three-quarters of 18- to 25-year-olds had received financial help from parents in the previous year, and nearly two-thirds said parents had assisted with errands, housework, and home repairs.

The trophy kids remain much closer for much longer to their doting parents than earlier generations and generally enjoy better relationships with their families and other older adults. Even as the millennials head off to college and take jobs, their parents remain their trusted advisers. That is creating havoc in the workplace as some hovering "helicopter parents" try to get involved in job interviews, salary negotiations, and even performance reviews. Clearly, millennials and their parents need to strike a better balance so that this generation learns to think and act more independently.

A DARKER SIDE

Some researchers tend to glamorize millennials and gloss over the generation's negative attributes. True, many young people today are healthy and well adjusted, with resumes chock-full of accomplishments. But like any generation, millennials have their share of vices as well as virtues. Some millennials engage in such unhealthy activities as binge drinking, abuse of both illegal and prescription drugs, and sexual promiscuity.

Research studies assessing the problems yield mixed results. According to the Centers for Disease Control and

Prevention's (CDC's) National Youth Risk Behavior Survey, the rates of sexual activity and alcohol and drug use have declined in recent years among high school students. Even so, a CDC study in 2008 estimated that one in four teenage girls is infected with at least one sexually transmitted disease. What's more, the Partnership for a Drug Free America's teen tracking study found that one in five had abused a prescription pain medication, and a similar number had abused prescription stimulants and tranquilizers. The partnership dubbed today's teens Generation Rx.

When the Pew Research Center asked an older group— 18- to 25-year-olds—about negative behaviors, roughly 70% said they believe their generation engages more in violence to solve conflicts and more in binge drinking than young adults did 20 years ago. About 63% said their generation is illegally using drugs more, and three-quarters said casual sex is more prevalent. Indeed, older generations are especially critical of millennials for their emotionally uninvolved hook-ups and sexual relationships with "friends with benefits."

There is also a downside to the millennial generation's competitive drive. When Harris Interactive surveyed 8- to 21-year-olds in 2007, they said they worry more about getting good grades than anything else. This obsession with grades is leading some young millennials to become stressed out, anxious, and sleep deprived. Teachers also complain that in their quest to win admission to the most elite universities, millennials are much more concerned about high marks than about learning and enrichment.

Perhaps because of the intense pressure to succeed academically, cheating is widespread among twentysomethings. In a 2006 study of 32 graduate schools in the United States and Canada, researchers at Pennsylvania State University, Rutgers University, and Washington State University found that 56% of business school students admitted to cheating at least once in the previous academic year, as did 47% of non-business students. Although millennials contend that they want to work for companies with integrity, many of them apparently aren't living up to such high ethical standards themselves.

BENETTON GENERATION

As more millennials move into the workplace, it's starting to resemble a Benetton advertisement of many colors and cultures. Because this is such an ethnically and racially mixed generation, it could signal major strides in diversifying the middle and upper management ranks of corporate America. In a study of U.S. college freshman trends, the Higher Education Research Institute at the University of California at Los Angeles found particularly sharp jumps in the proportion of Asian students, 8.6% in 2006, compared with 0.6% in 1971, and Latino students, 7.3%, up from 0.6%. Over the same period, the share of white students fell from 90.9% to 76.5%.

There is also a gender shift under way, with girls and young women accounting for a growing share of college and graduate school enrollments and taking on more leadership roles in companies. According to the UCLA freshman study, 55% of students are now women.

Having grown up with greater diversity in their neighborhoods and schools, millennials tend to be more open and accepting of each other, regardless of gender, color, religion, or sexual orientation. Multiracial and multicultural friendships are commonplace. UCLA reports that in its 2007 freshman survey, 37% of students said that helping promote racial understanding is a personal goal of theirs, the highest level since 1994.

Millennials also are more positive than older generations about such divisive social issues as gay marriage, interracial dating, and immigration. The Pew Research Center found that 47% of 18- to 25-year-olds favor legalization of gay marriage, compared with only 30% of people over 25. Similarly, 61% of the younger group believes that gays and lesbians should be able to adopt children, whereas only 44% of older people concur.

As for interracial dating, 89% of 18- to 25-year-olds consider it acceptable, whereas 70% of people over 25 approve. And when asked whether the growing number of immigrants strengthens American society, two-thirds of 18- to 25-year-olds said yes, compared with 57% of 26- to 40-year-olds, 47% of 41- to 60-year-olds, and 38% of those over 60.

To be sure, there are still class and cultural differences among the millennials. But the racial and ethnic tensions are likely to be much less pronounced with this generation than with older Americans. Millennials favor a corporate culture of inclusion and tolerance and will gravitate toward companies that actively promote racial and cultural diversity. "We're finding young people we hire much more progressive on workplace issues," says William Margaritis, the head of corporate communications and investor relations at FedEx Corp. "They want to know up front about a company's commitment to diversity."

Danielle Beyer certainly does. She graduated from a high school with dozens of nationalities and then attended the internationally diverse University of Rochester in New York. "At a time when whom you do business with is no longer limited by countries' borders, a diverse workforce is important to me," says Beyer, who joined the financial services company National City Corp. after receiving her M.B.A. degree from Rochester. "I've always liked having the opportunity to ask a peer or coworker about the places they've been and how they got to where they are today."

Beyond the cultural diversity within their own ranks, the millennials also have developed a worldliness that will serve them well in the increasingly global economy. These days, recruiters say, it's the rare resume from a millennial that doesn't include at least a summer of study overseas, as well as volunteer work in developing nations, interesting pleasure trips to exotic lands, and fluency in at least one foreign language. In the 2007 UCLA study of freshmen, 52% said they were interested in understanding other cultures and countries better, up from 43% in 2002. And in Harris Interactive's youth study, 8- to 21-year-olds listed traveling the world and speaking another language as their top two ambitions.

"It used to be unusual to see students who had taught in other countries or been involved in groups like the Peace Corps or Habitat for Humanity, but now we're interviewing many with international experiences that amount to much more than just vacations abroad," says John Ventola, cochairman of the hiring committee and summer program at the law firm Choate, Hall & Stewart in Boston. "Their open-minded view of the world is a very valuable attribute for lawyers, who shouldn't think about things rigidly but should take into account different viewpoints. That's what diversity is really all about."

MILLENNIALS AROUND THE GLOBE

Although the millennial generation is identified most closely with the United States, teenagers and young adults in other countries share many of the same attributes as their American counterparts.

De Wazières, the recruiting chief at L'Oréal, has noticed that millennials around the globe are surprisingly similar. "One thing I find to be very universal is that they have international experiences, are eager to take on the world, and value their relationships with their parents and the relationships they can develop with older people in the workplace," he says. "I tell our managers the good news is that this generation won't hate you."

He particularly observes the common bonds between millennials of different cultures at L'Oréal's annual marketing and strategy competitions for business school students. "It's the best way to witness how alike this generation is, whether they're from Malaysia, India, France, Argentina, or the United States," he says. "They wear the same clothing, have the same iPods, and mix and connect easily. Two hours after meeting, they're probably best friends on Facebook." Indeed, this is clearly a high-tech generation, regardless of geography. Technology has linked young people from all corners of the globe and allowed them to share information and experiences virtually.

"There are cultural and geographic differences that cause things to play out a little differently," says Atkinson, the management education consultant. "But I see many similarities across national boundaries in the millennials' optimism, manifest destiny to change the world, and drive to succeed."

Researchers in Australia, for example, have found millennials Down Under to be much like those in the United States on several counts, including their job-hopping habits. An Australian study by the recruiting firm Drake revealed that nearly two-thirds of millennials stay less than two years with an employer, and nearly half had already held five jobs in their few short years in the workplace.

Some studies have focused on millennials in several different countries and come up with striking parallels. The market-research firm Synovate looked at young people in the United Kingdom, Canada, and the United States and labeled them the "stay-at-home generation" because they tend to rely so much on parents for support and often live with them longer than previous generations. "The taboo of living with Mom and Dad has disappeared in a number of countries, not just the United States," says Julian Rolfe, global manager of syndicated youth research. "It has a lot to do with best friend parenting, especially with mothers and daughters who share clothes and music and think of each other as mates." In the United Kingdom, millennials who linger in the nest are sometimes called "kippers," short for "kids in parents' pockets eroding retirement savings."

PricewaterhouseCoopers undertook a major study of millennials in the United States, United Kingdom, and China to determine their expectations about work. In a survey of about 2,700 graduates who were offered jobs with the accounting firm, it found that more than 90% of millennials in all three countries believe they are more likely than their parents to "work across geographic borders," and roughly three-quarters believe they will have two to five employers during their careers. About 10% of the Chinese students expect to work for 10 or more employers, compared with 3% of the U.S. and U.K. respondents.

"This is a very demanding, very career savvy group of young people with huge similarities across countries," says Michael Rendell, partner and leader of human resource services for PricewaterhouseCoopers. "To keep them from leaving, companies will have to give them more responsibilities early in their careers and offer them a range of opportunities, including international assignments."

Despite such research studies, some educators and recruiting experts worry that millennials in the United States may find members of their generation from other countries, especially Asian nations, stiff competition because of a stronger work ethic. "We can expect the millennial generation's international counterparts from China, India, and other countries to pass them by in promotions, raises, and career development, while the American millennials are tending to their own personal needs," says Bruce Moore, associate director of the career management center at the Cox School of Business at Southern Methodist University in Dallas.

Dennis Garritan, director of graduate programs in human resource management at New York University, warns millennials to be especially concerned about competition from China. "I believe Chinese women in the millennial generation who are multilingual and intellectually gifted will give Americans a run for their money," he says. "They bring the millennials' skills, but they also have the baby boomers' work ethic. Personally, I would hate to have to compete with some of these young Chinese women for jobs."

CHAPTER HIGHLIGHTS

- Highly accomplished and doted on by their parents, the trophy kids are arriving in the workplace by the millions. Employers are benefiting from their technology, multitasking, and teamwork skills, but bristling at their demands for flexible working conditions, frequent feedback and guidance, and rapid promotion.

- Companies are struggling to integrate the millennial generation of trophy kids with three other distinctly different generations in the workplace—traditionalists, baby boomers, and generation Xers. Employers need to learn as much about the millennials as possible because like them or not, they represent the future workforce.

- Despite the insecurity of living in a world filled with terrorism threats and wars, the millennials remain an optimistic, confident generation. Self-absorbed and exhibitionistic, many millennials aspire to be rich and famous. Yet they also have an altruistic streak that leads many to perform community service.

- Millennials are explorers. They are inclined to change jobs frequently in their search for the ideal career, and many are delaying the milestones of adulthood— marriage, children, and home ownership.

- Millennials have vices as well as virtues, including alcohol and drug abuse, casual sex habits, and cheating in school.

- The millennial generation, a blend of colors and cultures, prefers to work for companies with a diverse workforce. Young people also are worldlier in their experiences and perspectives, a valuable asset in an increasingly global economy.

- Millennials around the world share many of the same characteristics, including their technology savvy, drive to succeed, job-hopping tendencies, and close connection to parents. But some career counselors worry that the stronger work ethic of millennials in some Asian countries may prove to be a competitive threat to young Americans, who are overly concerned about their personal needs and passions.

2

Great Expectations

When Gretchen Neels, a Boston-based consultant, was coaching a group of students for job interviews, she asked them how they believe employers view them. She gave them a clue, telling them that the word she was looking for begins with the letter *e*. One young man quickly shouted out, "excellent." Not that "e" word, she said. Soon other students chimed in with "enthusiastic" and "energetic." Not even close. The correct answer, she finally said, is "entitled." "Huh?" the students responded, surprised and even hurt to think that managers are offended by their highfalutin opinions of themselves.

"What is it with these girls? It's like generation Y gave way to generation I.D.—I Deserve," Zoe Burden told her husband on the television show *Cashmere Mafia*. The investment banker was fed up with the two narcissistic young women in her life—her nanny and her office assistant—who were bungling their jobs but still making excessive demands of her.

In a survey of corporate recruiters by *The Wall Street Journal* and Harris Interactive, that unflattering "e" word "entitled" and two more, "excessive expectations," popped up quite regularly in comments about the millennial generation. When asked how millennials are different from previous generations, survey respondents complained vehemently about their young recruits. A sampling of their comments:

> "Enormous sense of entitlement, less willingness to earn their keep."

> "Expect too much too soon; very self-centered."

> "Lazier, more entitled."

> "Want it all delivered to them on a silver platter."

> "So entitled they expect to fly up the corporate ladder."

> "They believe two years of experience is enough to run their own company."

If there's one overriding perception of millennials, it is that they are a generation with great—and sometimes outlandish—expectations. Although members of most generations were considered somewhat spoiled in their youth, many millennials feel an unusually strong sense of entitlement. Older adults routinely criticize the high-maintenance rookies for wanting too much too soon. In particular, they resent the impatient millennials for expecting overnight advancement from their entry-level jobs. "They want to be CEO tomorrow," is a common refrain from frustrated corporate recruiters. Whatever happened to paying your dues, they wonder. As Zoe of *Cashmere Mafia* put it, "When I was their age, we were so grateful to have a job and we were so aware of how expendable we were."

The "We Want It All" generation feels no such gratitude. It expects the workplace to adapt to its needs. That means loads of attention and near daily performance feedback from bosses. Millennials also want to learn as much as they can and have as many different experiences as possible. They love praise and count on getting regular promotions and pay raises. By "regular," they mean every six months or so like clockwork.

"Their attitude is always what are you going to give me," says Natalie Griffith, manager of human resource programs at Eaton Corp., an industrial manufacturer. "It's not necessarily arrogance; it's simply their mindset." But it can be a costly point of view. One job candidate was rejected after a second-round interview, when he asked what Eaton could do for him, rather than what he could contribute to the company.

"Once they're hired, they want the big stuff right off the bat," Griffith adds. "Coming out of leadership training, they'll shoot for higher salaries right away. One woman asked for higher wages because she felt she deserved them, given the reputation of the school she was coming from and the fact that she thought her college projects should be considered experience."

Veronica Woody, head of International Business Machines Corp.'s (IBM's) Extreme Blue internship program for elite engineering and M.B.A. students, finds expectations much higher than when she looked for a summer job. "I just wanted an internship to help with college expenses and to give me some experience," she says. "This generation of students has a lot more chutzpah. They want to work on cool things and emerging technology that could change the world."

That's not all the millennial generation wants. Its expectations include much more than collecting fat salaries and doing groundbreaking work. Millennials also seek a flexible work routine that allows them time for their family and personal interests. Being very civic minded, they believe employers should provide opportunities for them to volunteer for community service. While they're at the office, they'd like to be able to dress casually, plug into their iPods and social networks, communicate electronically rather than face-to-face, and have a little fun, too. Worst of all from an employer's perspective, millennials often resign after a year or two—maybe even sooner—if they don't feel that all of their myriad needs are being satisfied.

More than 85% of hiring managers and human resource executives said they feel that millennials have a stronger sense of entitlement than older workers, according to a survey by the online jobs site CareerBuilder.com. The generation's greatest expectations: higher pay (74% of respondents), flexible work schedules (61%), a promotion within a year (56%), and more vacation or personal time (50%).

"They really do seem to want everything, and I can't decide if it's an inability or an unwillingness to make trade-offs," says Derrick Bolton, assistant dean and M.B.A. admissions director at Stanford University's Graduate School of Business. "They want to be CEO, for example, but they say they don't want to give up time with their families. If millennials feel this way because they can't make up their minds, it's not a good thing. They have to make decisions if they expect to be leaders."

Some research studies indicate that the millennial generation's expectations stem from feelings of superiority. Michigan State University's Collegiate Employment Research Institute and MonsterTrak, an online careers site, conducted a joint research study of 18- to 28-year-olds and found that nearly half had moderate to high superiority beliefs about themselves. The superiority factor was measured by responses to such statements as "I deserve favors from others" and "I know that I have more natural talents than most."

The millennial generation may expect so much because they were never denied much. From the nursery onward, millennials were indulged and made to feel special by parents, coaches, and teachers. Their self-esteem seems to know no bounds. The National Institute on Media and the Family and the Minnesota PTA have even launched a statewide campaign encouraging parents and educators to start saying no to young people more often. They are urging parents to read and heed the advice in the book *No: Why Kids—of All Ages—Need to Hear It and Ways Parents Can Say It*, by David Walsh, president of the institute. The Minnesota campaign blames "discipline deficit disorder" for this generation's inflated expectations and feelings of entitlement.

For their part, millennials believe they are misunderstood. They feel that their confidence and ambition are being misread as narcissism and entitlement. They also believe that they can afford to be picky, with talent shortages looming as graying baby boomers retire or switch to part-time assignments. "They are finding that they have to adjust work around our lives instead of us adjusting our lives around work," a teenage blogger named Olivia writes on the Web site Xanga.com. "What other option do they have? We are hard working and utilize tools to get the job done. But we don't want to work more than 40 hours a week, and we want to wear clothes that are comfortable. We want to be able to spice up the dull workday by listening to our iPods. If corporate America doesn't like that, too bad. They don't have much of a choice because there are other jobs out there that will take us."

She may be right, but sometimes such confidence comes off as cockiness. To employers, arrogance is never attractive, a lesson that many millennials have failed to learn. Neels, the consultant in Boston, often sees smug behavior when she helps students prepare for their job search. When she was conducting an intern recruiting session with M.B.A. students at Harvard Business School, for example, a young man showed up five minutes late casually dressed in cargo pants. Then his cell phone rang. "I thought my head would explode," she says. "Who does this kid think he is?"

Some millennials feel so sure of themselves that they won't even adapt to corporate recruiting schedules. Wachovia Corp., the financial services company, encouraged undergraduates to come to its first "super day" of second-round interviews because most of its job openings might get filled then. Despite the risks of losing the chance to work for Wachovia, some students opted to wait for a later "super day" so they wouldn't miss homecoming weekend at their college.

"It's all about them," says a recruiter for investment banking firm Goldman Sachs Group Inc. "Some students today even complain that the people interviewing them aren't smart enough and haven't read their resumes closely enough. They get upset if a recruiter checks his BlackBerry during an interview and doesn't pay complete attention to them."

Indeed, these outspoken young people tend to be highly opinionated, and fearlessly challenge recruiters and bosses. Status and hierarchy don't impress them much, and they find bureaucracy simply maddening. They want to be treated like colleagues rather than subordinates and expect ready access to senior executives, even the CEO, to share their brilliant ideas. If they bump into the CEO and one of his clients in the elevator, they have no compunction about interrupting and proclaiming, "Hey, I have this great idea I've been meaning to talk to you about."

Many millennials also think nothing of e-mailing top executives and addressing them by their first names. Recruiters at such companies as Goldman Sachs and Amazon.com describe "student stalkers" who brashly fire off e-mails to everyone from the CEO on down, trying to get an inside track to a job. Wachovia even rescinded a job offer to a student who e-mailed the company's top executives because he wouldn't accept the answers he had received from a recruiter and a hiring manager about tuition reimbursement policies.

The millennials' overly familiar behavior makes some older executives bristle. The owner of a public relations agency says it bothers her when her young female employees touch her arm or shoulder as if she's one of their girlfriends. Millennials may not mean to be rude, but their casualness clearly indicates that they don't recognize that age and experience command a certain level of respect.

MERITOCRACY FOR MILLENNIALS

There is little that millennials detest more than a rigid timetable for career advancement. The millennials have world-conquering ambition and don't want to feel constrained in the slightest. They want a true meritocracy that rewards performance regardless of years of seniority. That attitude, of course, doesn't fly at many law firms, investment banks, and other employers.

The millennials' belief in meritocracy should square quite nicely with the American ideal of achieving success through pluck and initiative. It's just that corporate hierarchies, union seniority rules, office politics, and other workplace dynamics sometimes interfere with the millennials' lofty goals.

Luke McGee, a senior analyst in investment banking at Merrill Lynch & Co., put in 15 hours or more a day and spent weekends at the office after joining the firm in 2005. So far, the Duke University graduate feels that the brutal schedule is paying off. He has been allowed to interact more directly with clients, which has helped sharpen his communication and presentation skills. "Despite my junior status and relatively short tenure here, I am often asked to express my view," he says. "The fact that senior bankers trust my ability to speak lucidly in front of clients and that they think I have a differentiated point of view is something I greatly appreciate."

Still, he wrestles with his frustration over the time it will take to rise to the level of managing director. "In a perfect world, Merrill would be a complete meritocracy in which seniority played much less of a role," he says. "I recognize that experience matters, and there is something to be said for having seen many things. However, I feel strongly that different bankers develop at different paces, and those who excel should be both advanced and compensated according to ability."

McGee has talked with colleagues about the long road to managing director and found some sympathy for his perspective. "I can't say that I have been completely satisfied with the response, but I appreciate that I have been able to have candid conversations," he says. "It's my hope that the system will at some point be less rigid. However, I realize that this career path is almost identical to the rest of Wall Street, so it's an industry issue."

Will McGee wait his turn at Merrill? He isn't making any promises. "I would like to think I can have a long-term career at Merrill," he says. "At some point, I can see myself wanting to take on new challenges. If those new challenges are available at Merrill, I will obviously explore the opportunity to stay here. If, for whatever reason, the fit isn't right at Merrill, I'll move on."

Not all companies adhere to lockstep promotion tracks. Millennials like McGee would likely feel less impatient at the Oliver Wyman management consulting firm. "We are a true meritocracy where people can progress rapidly to partner, often in as little as six years from their undergraduate education and without the need for an advanced degree," says Matthew Bennett, director of global recruiting. "This generation wants a place where progression is measured with a speedometer, not an odometer, and where there are no artificial ceilings on career movement."

Oliver Wyman finds that its promise "to get people there faster" resonates strongly with millennial students, as does the prospect of gaining access to senior colleagues and clients very early in their careers. "While they don't expect to be cracking the problem all the time," Bennett says, "they want to sit at the table when it is being done rather than sit in a cubicle somewhere cranking out analyses."

MOBILE MILLENNIALS

Although millennials have high expectations about what their employers should provide them, companies shouldn't expect much loyalty in return. Because of their grand expectations, most millennials have no intention of settling down for long with one employer. They always have one foot out the door, looking ahead to the next big career move. If a job doesn't prove fulfilling, they will forsake it in a flash.

Indeed, many employers say that recruiting millennials isn't their biggest challenge. It's retention that worries them most. After companies invest thousands of dollars in recruiting and training, they shudder to see their young up-and-comers suddenly bolt to another employer. "These young people are going to break your heart, so don't get personally invested in them," says Marilyn Moats Kennedy, a consultant on workplace issues. "They know there are other opportunities and don't mind having a series of short-term jobs."

In the *Wall Street Journal*/Harris Interactive survey of corporate recruiters, fully half of the respondents said it is becoming increasingly difficult to retain the transient millennial generation. "They are unwilling to stick out tough situations that take more time to solve than they are willing to give," one recruiter said. "They will job-hop without thinking about the consequences to their careers." Another commented, "This generation is very fickle. They are not necessarily looking for a career relationship with a company."

Millennials want their dream job as early as possible, but entry-level positions are seldom dream jobs. As young people encounter the realities of the workaday world, many are quickly disillusioned and want to continue exploring to get it right. In essence, the millennials operate as free agents who can bounce from one job to the next anytime they choose. They place a premium on self-determination and want to be in charge of their careers. Their aim is to develop as many marketable skills as possible, and they expect companies to help them with their resume-building mission, even though they'll probably jump ship after a few years. In the Michigan State/MonsterTrak study, about two-thirds of the millennials said they would likely "surf" from one job to the next. In addition, about 44% showed their lack of loyalty by stating that they would renege on a job acceptance commitment if a better offer came along.

The disloyalty is understandable. Many millennials have seen family members laid off through corporate downsizings or outsourcing of jobs to other countries. They know job security vanished long ago from the workplace, so they want to be prepared to change career paths throughout their lives. From their perspective, their lack of commitment is simply a survival strategy.

Millennials do feel some degree of loyalty, but it's toward the individuals they work with, not the faceless organizations that pay their salaries. Ultimately, many of them may end up dropping out of corporate life altogether and going the entrepreneurial route. That's what Justin Pfister did. After working in information technology for a subsidiary of Time Warner Inc., he became discouraged and left to work full-time on his start-up Open Yard, an online retailer of sports equipment. In his corporate job, he says, "It was very clear that the business roles seemed afraid of the IT people who think creatively and implement their own ideas. I was constantly told my ideas were good, but nothing came of them because the business lacked understanding of the issues, such as mobile phone technology and Web service generation."

Pfister believes that the millennial generation will resist being pigeonholed and having their expectations deflated. "We can sing, dance, and write our own music," he declares. "We get stifled when we're offered single-dimensional jobs. We are multidimensional people living and working in a multi-dimensional world."

Millennials are quite candid in chatting about their career goals and their desire to move on after gaining some experience at their current employer. Young professionals at several companies freely shared with me their plans to leave within a few years, even though they were being interviewed at their corporate offices. Other generations might have been reluctant to openly discuss their focus on personal goals rather than long-term loyalty to their company. But most millennials have no such qualms.

Two millennial professionals I met at Ernst & Young are content in their jobs for now, but both have bigger dreams that may ultimately mean leaving the accounting firm. Although Lena Licata enjoys her work in the technology and information services practice, she considered quitting after she hit the two-year mark. "Job switching is definitely a characteristic of my generation," she says. "After two years in a job, many of my friends felt they had to move on to another company or go back to school. But I decided to stay put because of the variety of assignments I was getting and the opportunities I had to switch to other groups within the firm to acquire new skills."

Still, Ernst & Young isn't likely to be her final career destination, and Licata doesn't feel the least bit disloyal in acknowledging it. Her career vision: owning her own horse farm. "I would like in a few years to use the firm's flexible work arrangements and my income to put together a farm," she says, "then have a family and run my own business." Even before attending Lehigh University, she flirted with the idea of becoming a riding instructor instead. But, she recalls, "My dad asked me, 'Don't you want to own the barn, not just work in the barn?'"

Devin Duffy, an Ernst & Young colleague who works in the transaction real estate group, also ponders possible future moves. Like many young professionals, he is considering going to business school for an M.B.A. degree, after which real estate opportunity funds could be on the horizon. "What matters most to me now is the breadth of experiences I can have at Ernst & Young," he says. "The exit options are greater if my learning trajectory here doesn't flatten out."

Some of his frustrated friends in the finance and real estate industries have told him they are getting stuck with monotonous tasks a year or two after graduation. But thus far, Duffy still feels as if he is growing and outpacing his peers. He has received top performance ratings, pay raises, and bonuses, and he felt honored to participate in Ernst & Young's global branding strategy initiative and to be profiled in a video on its careers Web site. "I continue to have high expectations for myself and my career wherever it may lead," says the University of Wisconsin graduate.

Of course, few people of any age today expect to spend a lifetime in the same career with the same employer. But millennials are an unusually mobile group. These workplace nomads don't see any stigma in listing three different jobs in a single year on their resumes. They are quite confident about landing yet another new job. In the meantime, they needn't worry about their next paycheck because they have their parents to cushion them. They're comfortable in the knowledge that they can move back home for an indefinite amount of time while they seek another job.

When recruiters question the gaps in their resumes, millennials don't have any reservations about simply saying, "Well, the job just didn't work out," or "I needed a break and wanted to travel." In fact, some millennials view their job switching as an asset. Nearly half of 18- to 24-year-olds said they were likely to leave their employers in the next year, and 61% said they believe they increase their career potential by periodically switching jobs, according to a study by the recruiting firm Spherion Corp.

Still, companies understandably are leery of job hoppers whose resumes list three or four different employers within a year or two. They may bring a variety of experience, but such frequent career moves still won't be a selling point with many companies. Corporate recruiters and college career services directors advise millennials to try to be less impatient and impetuous. In due time, the promotions will come, and while they wait, they will be acquiring valuable new skills and experiences. Millennials also might be wise to ask themselves if there really is a better job waiting for them elsewhere.

Such counsel may fall on deaf ears. But recruiters can also consider trying to recapture talented millennials who stray and later regret their hasty departure. "I believe that recapture is more important than retention with this new generation," says Kennedy, the consultant. "Let them go, wait six months, then call and tell them if they don't like what they're doing, they can come back."

Johnson & Johnson believes in following that strategy, too. "Older generations valued staying at a company for 30 years, but I understand that this young generation wants to grow and develop through a variety of experiences," says Kaye Foster-Cheek, vice president for human resources. "If valuable people leave, we will reconnect with them in a few years and try to re-recruit them."

MANAGING EXPECTATIONS

Even if the millennial generation's expectations are exasperating, companies certainly have a vested interest in trying to increase their retention rate and slow down the millennial mobility rate. They not only will need this generation to fill positions left vacant by retiring baby boomers but also can benefit from this generation's best and brightest, who possess significant strengths in teamwork, technology skills, social networking, and multitasking. Millennials were bred for achievement by success-driven parents, and most will work hard as long as the task at hand is engaging and promises a tangible payoff.

"We all want to feel valued and get rewarded in the workplace; the millennials are just more vocal about wanting it," says Gail McDaniel, a corporate consultant and career coach for college students. "Companies need to understand that something's gotta give here. If they behave the same as they have the past 40 years, they won't have people to run their operations down the road."

The trick is to manage the millennials' expectations in a way that pays off for both employee and employer. Clearly, companies that want to compete for top talent must bend a bit and adapt to the millennial generation in some important ways, such as by offering frequent performance appraisals and flexibility in work schedules. No doubt, it will be a Herculean challenge to keep this generation motivated, but companies can adjust their management approach to make millennials feel engaged, not alienated. Here are some strategies that should help keep the millennials happy:

- For starters, show new hires how their work makes a difference and why it's of value to the company. Millennials have a low threshold for boredom, and flourish in challenging assignments that give them a sense of accomplishment. Even if a chore seems mundane, managers can explain why it's meaningful and critical to the long-term success of a project.

- Never try to bully millennials. They don't like an authoritarian, command-and-control style of management that makes them feel subservient. They prefer a collaborative, team-oriented environment in which they can be heard and can feel that their views truly matter. Smart managers will listen to their opinions, show respect for their insights, and give them some say in decision making.

- Don't tell millennials that they'll have a job for life with your company. That will sound like a death sentence to the instant messaging generation. What they do want to know is how fast they can advance. So be very clear in explaining their responsibilities and how meeting them will spur their careers along. Short of a major promotion, companies can add responsibilities and upgrade job titles to show career progress. Employers also can detail the variety of career opportunities available to millennials if they'll just stick around awhile and demonstrate their worth.

Indeed, it's the wealth of opportunities that will prove to be the most effective retention tool. "We find it's a huge retention benefit that young employees can switch jobs every year or two, but still stay at IBM," says Rachel Robards, a diversity programs manager.

Rick Genett, marketing manager for WebSphere Commerce, finds IBM's "opportunity marketplace" jobs site "an invaluable tool to not only see what assignments are open, but also keep a pulse on what they require in terms of experience and skills." He also has arranged informal interviews to introduce himself to executives and learn more about other groups within IBM. That's how he landed his current post, which counts as his fifth job in his five years with the company. "My parents, especially my mother, have trouble grasping that many jobs in just five years," Genett says. "To them, a steady paycheck is what matters. But it takes more than pay to keep me and my generation engaged. It takes feedback, praise, and new responsibilities and opportunities."

International experiences also can help win the allegiance of millennials. Some young people today expect a temporary overseas assignment earlier in their careers than previous generations. In fact, many millennials already have traveled and studied abroad before entering the corporate world.

When managers at KPMG asked a group of about 600 interns how many have passports, virtually all of them raised their hands. That didn't surprise Manny Fernandez, national managing partner for university relations and recruiting. He sees the accounting firm's international opportunities as one of its best retention tools. For example, young tax professionals can take advantage of KPMG's Tax Trek program, which offers a three-month international placement. "We are unusual in that we offer global experiences to interns and new hires during their first year with us," he says. "Waiting five years for an international assignment is like a lifetime to this generation."

Managing expectations, however, isn't all about accommodating the millennials. The millennials sometimes need a little taming. They must make trade-offs and conform to some degree to the corporate culture, even if that means forgoing jeans and flip-flops for dresses and suits and attending meetings in the flesh rather than virtually.

One of the best lessons millennials could learn is how to adjust their expectations to the plateaus of workplace life. Even the most exciting job has some routine aspects to it, and millennials need to show more patience for tasks they consider menial. They really can't have it all, at least not all the time.

When prima donnas get out of line, Deborah Holmes, director of corporate social responsibility at Ernst & Young, tries to be understanding. But sometimes she has to make it clear who's in charge. "Millennials will say, 'I find this part of the project boring and don't want to do it,'" she says. "And I respond, 'Well, I'm glad to know how you feel, but it's still an important skill that you need to develop.'"

Before millennials even land their first jobs, parents should provide a reality check to balance their expectations. Although it's wonderful to foster self-esteem and tell children to shoot for the moon, responsible parents also need to point out that jobs are demanding, discouraging, and dull, as well as challenging, fun, and exciting. They probably can get the message across best through example, by relating their own personal tales about the glories and the horrors of the workplace.

College career placement offices also can help tone down expectations by preparing millennials for compromises they'll need to make in the workplace. Patty Phillips, executive director of career management at the Simon Graduate School of Business at the University of Rochester, believes that her office must act more as a "shock absorber" between the world of work and the more protective nest of academia. "The better job we can do," she says, "the smoother the transition."

Phillips feels the need to advise students on some pretty basic behavior: shut your laptops when you're spoken to, arrive at work on time, and dress appropriately. "We might have a student with five earrings who won't work for a company that judges people on appearance," she says. "I suggest that the student take them out, get into the company, do a great job, and then put all five earrings back in."

Bruce Moore, associate director of the career management center at the Cox School of Business at Southern Methodist University, also tries to impart some workplace wisdom to millennial students who are myopically focused on their dreams. "What I try to teach—or preach—to my 'special students' is that it's not all about you and that in the real world, the focus will be on the team, the project, the company goals," he says. "They need to understand that they will have to adjust, or they are going to have a very difficult time successfully integrating and advancing."

GENERATIONAL COUNSELING

With four generations in the workplace at the same time, companies worry about how well their employees will mesh. Clearly, there's animosity among the generations, which include the millennials, generation Xers, baby boomers, and traditionalists. The older generations tend to write off millennials as a bunch of whiners who not only expect too much but also lack a strong work ethic. From their elders' perspective, millennials aren't as loyal and dependable as traditionalists, aren't willing to earn their stripes as work-centric baby boomers did, and are less self-reliant than generation X.

Here's what a 63-year-old critic had to say about the millennials in an e-mail to me after one of my articles appeared in *The Wall Street Journal:* "The lucky schools and employers will be those who fail to attract these spoiled millennial babies until they are knocked around enough to realize that the world is not going to give them the sort of support and detailed guidance they expect."

Cindy Rakowitz, a public relations executive in Encino, California, is similarly put off by the millennials. "They are very ego driven and try to get away with putting in as little time as possible to complete their work," she says. "They make excuses about arriving late to the office without any guilt. Self-fulfillment comes first with them, responsibility later."

Millennials aren't any nicer in their comments about their elders. On *The Wall Street Journal*'s Law Blog, for example, millennials call law firm partners "old fogies" and declare, "All you boomers need to do us a favor and die."

To be sure, some young people do respect the experience and institutional knowledge of their elders. Pfister, the founder of Open Yard, acknowledges that there's "a disconnect" between millennials and older generations. "I don't sense a lot of respect from them for our work ethics and ideas," he says. Still, he adds that he considers older workers "our most valuable asset because they can teach us a lot and save us a ton of time and mistakes. My aged mentors have been the biggest help. I've seen some older, very successful people break down and talk to me about their inadequacies and tell me what they thought was truly important."

By tapping the different perspectives and experiences of the four generations, companies can gain valuable insights. Yet how do they prevent dissension and overcome the generational bias? It's a very tall order but an absolute priority as the generational makeup of the workplace continues to shift. The generations are likely to collide for many years to come, so it's best to start minimizing the damage now.

Companies should first encourage greater understanding through more open, honest communication. They need to teach the generations to try to appreciate their different abilities, attitudes, and styles of working rather than take a dismissive view of each other. Team-building activities and mentoring can certainly help. Not only can older managers provide guidance and share their many years of accumulated knowledge with millennials, but young people also can teach their elders a thing or two about new technologies and online social networking.

For Michael Kannisto, global staffing director at contact lens maker Bausch & Lomb Inc., the best strategy is to introduce this "new species" into the workplace in very small doses, followed by conversations with older generations after they have interacted with a few millennials. "I'm seeing some real disconnects between young people who do phenomenal work and boomer bosses who can't get past feeling that they didn't like the slides or the way the young people dressed or the way they talked or the way they presented their conclusions," says Kannisto, who reminds older managers that in 5 to 10 years they may be begging millennials to work for Bausch & Lomb. "It's not about making the older generations like the millennials; it's about educating people to the differences."

At the same time, he understands why some bosses resent millennials. When a group of college seniors visited Bausch & Lomb, they were asked where they would like to work if they could choose any company in the world. They rattled off names like Google and Starbucks, but "no one threw us a bone and said Bausch & Lomb," Kannisto recalls. "After their visit, we received one thank-you note—from the students' baby-boomer teacher. That was another example to me of this generation's self-centeredness."

To keep the peace, some employers are trying to stimulate more dialogue through generational insights workshops. The training programs attempt to dispel unfair stereotypes and prevent misunderstandings. Such seminars are similar to diversity training sessions that promote harmony among workers of different genders, racial and ethnic backgrounds, and sexual orientations.

Companies are especially hoping they can help the older generations better understand the millennials' expectations about work. One of the most common generational conflicts is over the number of hours worked in the office. Millennials feel that they should be measured by the quantity and quality of work completed, regardless of when and where it's done. But older managers believe strongly in punctuality and plenty of face time. A major corporate recruiter was amazed by one of his young M.B.A. hires who wanted to take long lunch hours to do her banking and spend a few hours a day shopping online and surfing the Internet. She said going online made her feel good and helped break up the stressful workday.

Such generational clashes don't surprise Diane Piktialis, research working group and project leader for the Conference Board, a business research organization in New York City. "Older workers who grew up in a face-time culture believe young people have no work ethic if they leave at five o'clock," she says. "What they don't realize is that the millennial worker gets online and is working at home at midnight."

Piktialis was a speaker at a generational diversity training session at IBM, which hopes to resolve some of the differences among its employees over work and management styles and familiarity with technology. Among the issues discussed at the event: millennials' need for more frequent feedback than annual or semiannual reviews, their tendency to approach senior managers without regard for hierarchy, and their demands for work-life balance.

Similarly, Merrill Lynch managers are participating in seminars called "Uncommon Threads: Four Generations in the Workplace." As part of the program, managers are asked if they would give an employee time off because he says he's sick. Of course they would. What if he asked for time off to visit his spiritual adviser? Their first reaction: "What is a spiritual adviser?" followed by disbelief. The point of that exercise, of course, is that the millennials will expect flexible hours for personal needs that many older generations won't consider valid reasons to take time off. "Managers absolutely need to understand the millennials better," says Subha Barry, managing director and head of global diversity and inclusion at Merrill Lynch. "They are going to force us to change a bit for them."

For Ernst & Young, the millennial generation is also serious business. By 2010, the accounting firm expects it to account for more than half of its client-serving employees, up from 32% in 2007. Even so, the company takes a somewhat lighter approach in its generational dynamics workshops for interns, new hires, and managers. Called "Hello. WU?! [text-message lingo for What's up?]: Your Pocket Guide to Generational Differences," the presentation even includes quizzes and prizes. At the workshops, employees learn characteristics of the baby boomers (materialist "me generation"), generation X (realistic, cynical), and generation Y or the millennials (instant gratification). They also are advised to develop their "emotional intelligence" by acknowledging their own needs and respecting those of the other generations.

Goldman Sachs is also dealing with the generation gap creatively. The investment banking firm enlists actors to portray millennials who assertively seek more feedback, responsibility, and involvement in decision making from their baby boomer and gen X managers and teammates. After the performance, employees discuss and debate the generational differences they have seen played out.

In the final analysis, the generational tension is a bit ironic. After all, the grumbling baby-boomer managers are the same indulgent, overly protective parents who produced the millennial generation with its grandiose expectations. But oddly, the boomers can't seem to relate to these alien millennials when they reach the workplace.

"We need to get the boomers to recognize that they should treat younger workers as they handled their children in the home environment," says Roy Schroer, assistant vice president for recruitment at Union Pacific Corp., the railroad operator. "Are they as caring and protective of junior employees as they are of their own children? Is the management style they use at work the same as the management style at home?"

Barry of Merrill Lynch also gets the irony. She is teaching her teenage daughter to value her own opinions and to challenge things. Now she sees many of those challenging millennials streaming into her company and wonders how she and other managers can expect the kids they raised to suddenly behave differently at work.

"It doesn't mean we can be as indulgent as managers as we are as parents; we have to slap them back a little," she says. "But as parents of young people just like them, we can treat them with respect. Maybe they can't sit in and listen to the presentation they helped put together for senior management. But we can tell them, 'If not this time, maybe you can next time.'"

CHAPTER HIGHLIGHTS

- A strong sense of entitlement is one of the most striking characteristics of the millennial generation. Young people have extremely high expectations about their jobs—everything from a desire for frequent performance feedback and fast promotions to a need for work-life balance and opportunities to perform community service.

- Millennials gravitate toward employers with a culture of meritocracy. They want to advance as quickly as their achievements merit, and they absolutely detest any rigid timetables hampering their rise to the top.

- Because of their great expectations, millennials are notoriously fickle and prone to job hopping. In fact, some employers consider retention a bigger challenge than recruiting this young generation.

- To improve their retention rates, companies must work harder to keep millennials engaged in their jobs. That means clearly showing them the value and impact of their work, creating a collegial and team-oriented culture, and, above all, offering them a rich variety of opportunities to advance their careers.

- Millennials, of course, need to temper their expectations and meet employers halfway. Parents and college advisers can help by urging young people to behave respectfully, dress appropriately, and learn to cope with the routine, boring parts of their jobs.

- The millennials and the three other generations in the workplace are colliding, forcing employers to try to reduce the level of bias and resentment. Some companies are organizing seminars to open the lines of communication and help the generations better understand differences in their attitudes and styles of working.

3

Apron
Strings

To Dwayne McClelland, it's simply his fatherly duty to do all he can to help his children. So when his son faced a scheduling conflict for a meeting with faculty advisers in mechanical engineering and petroleum engineering at Texas A&M University, McClelland showed up alone to ask questions on his behalf. The advisers found it a bit amusing and remarked that this was a first for them, seeing a parent arrive without the prospective student.

McClelland's support didn't stop there. He also provided "editorial support and content suggestions" for his son's admission essays and scholarship applications. Because his son applied to only one university, he explains, "it was imperative that he put his best foot forward to ensure admittance." He later intervened to persuade the university to change its decision denying his son credit for a community college scuba diving course. "My son was not sufficiently mature and confident to buck administrative bureaucracy," he says. "I needed to step in to champion his cause, in the process teaching him that just because something is decided by an authority figure doesn't always make it right."

To McClelland, what millennials need are parents who will keep them on track, whether meeting deadlines for college applications or representing them at an important meeting with university professors. "They don't always understand the importance of deadlines and attention to detail," he says. "They'd rather go off and have fun."

McClelland, a petroleum engineer for Chevron Corp., acknowledges that he may qualify as a "helicopter parent," but he feels no need to make excuses. "I take exception to the belief that so-called helicopter parenting is necessarily a bad thing," he says. "In moderation, I believe it actually can serve the best interests of both the child and the parents. Parents are meant to help their children in the transition from young adulthood to full independence, and I for one intend to continue to do just that."

McClelland sees himself helping his son navigate through college and then the oil industry. "He can benefit from my mistakes and what I have learned," he explains. "Obviously, I will use my insider knowledge to steer my son to the right job; my benefit to him will be in helping him marry his interests with the corporate culture that best suits them." McClelland stresses that he wouldn't think of attending a job interview with his son, as some parents are attempting to do these days. "My son is fully capable of coming across well in an interview," he says, but then adds that he expects to coach his son on interviewing strategies "because he's kind of shy."

It used to be that Mom cried and Dad winced as they put their darling on the bus to college and finally cut the apron strings. No longer. Today, helicopter parents continue to stay intimately involved with their millennial generation kids long after they leave home for college—and even after they embark on their careers. Many college students and twentysomething workers tell me that they communicate with their parents at least once daily. In past generations, parents were lucky if they heard from their kids once a week. But this is clearly the tethered generation. For millennials, the cell phone has become the new high-tech umbilical cord. E-mail and text and instant messaging also contribute to the more frequent contact between parents and their grown children.

In one sense, children are growing up faster, putting away toys sooner and quickly adopting technology. Even preschoolers carry cell phones and portable video-game players. But they are maturing more slowly in other ways. Millennials are buying homes, marrying, and having children later than previous generations. They are even getting driver's licenses later, partly because parents are willing to chauffeur them around and are in no hurry to see their precious children driving on hazardous highways.

It is important that colleges and companies understand these parents who play such a key role in the daily lives of this generation. Their style of parenting helps explain some of the millennials' expectations and attitudes. The constant parental support has created a generation that needs constant feedback and direction in school and the workplace. Colleges are increasingly dealing with helicopter parents, and more companies also are being contacted directly by the parents of some of their millennial employees. The more both educators and employers know about what drives these parents, the better equipped they will be to handle them appropriately.

MEET THE PARENTS

First, some background on the much-maligned helicopter parents. They are so named because they hover like helicopters near their children, ready to swoop in at a moment's notice to help resolve problems big and small. Particularly militant helicopter parents have been dubbed Black Hawks. Those who keep their distance and just offer guidance and direction are labeled traffic-control helicopter parents.

Hovering parents aren't just an American phenomenon. In Sweden, for instance, overprotective parenting is called "curling," a reference to the sport of curling. In curling, players sweep the ice with brooms to remove obstacles and make the heavy stones speed toward the target area. Likewise, curling parents rush ahead of their children, sweeping their paths clean of even the smallest obstructions to make their lives easier.

Helicopter parenting requires dedication and time management skills. From the crib to the college dorm, helicopter parents dote on their children and micromanage their lives. They ferry them from play dates to soccer practice to music lessons, always making their children the focus of their lives. A 2008 television commercial for the Chevrolet Malibu nicely captures the millennial parents' deep concern for their children's welfare. Promoting the car as a safe vehicle that will continue to protect the child long after she leaves home, the ad opens with a cuddly baby crawling on an assembly line conveyer belt and progresses through childhood to proms and graduation. As the parents lovingly look on, robotic arms put a bicycle helmet on the little girl and a bandage on her skinned knee after a skateboarding mishap. Finally, the robots strap her in the driver's seat of a Malibu, and her parents watch her drive off into the future. The closing lines of the commercial: "Because safety should last a lifetime. The all-new Chevy Malibu: built to last, built to love."

We don't have to watch television, however, to recognize these proud, protective parents. We have all encountered them in our daily lives. They're the folks with those yellow "Baby on Board" signs in the rear window and bumper stickers asking, "Have you hugged your child today?" and declaring, "My child is a middle school honor student." They tangle with sports coaches whenever their child gets benched, sometimes nearly coming to blows and being ejected from the game. They're the nightmares of many a schoolteacher, berating them over every less than perfect report card and every stern disciplinary action. Teachers tell of parents who beg them to let their children redo term papers after being caught cheating and plagiarizing. Just how out of control are some helicopter parents getting? Roughly 60% of teachers responding to a 2007 job satisfaction survey in Howard County, Maryland, said parents had harassed them.

Helicopter parents help write their kids' application essays to vie for spots at the most elite universities. They may even accompany their children to admissions interviews, dominating the meeting with their own questions. A 2006 survey by College Parents of America, an advocacy organization for parents, found that 88% of prospective college parents expected to go on campus visits, 85% would help their children decide where to apply, 69% would be involved in drafting the applications, and nearly half would arrange for a prep course or tutoring for the SAT or ACT entrance exams. The message of the study is quite clear: today, colleges are recruiting families, not just students.

Once the acceptance letter arrives in the mailbox, parents next go to bat to get their children the best class schedules, housing, and roommate assignments. Then comes the separation anxiety. "We have parents who want to stay in campus residential facilities the first night or two after their children come to campus," says Jo-Anne Brady, registrar at Queen's University in Kingston, Ontario. "Our answer has been 'no,' but we know that many parents are staying anyway in local hotel accommodations." Some students have chosen to spend their first year abroad at the university's international study center in England, and a few concerned parents have even flown across the Atlantic to spend time with their children as they settle in.

Helicopter parenting is expected to intensify. "Future college parents believe they will have much greater levels of concern on nearly every topic from health and safety to finances, academics, and even personal relationships," says James Boyle, president of College Parents of America. "These soon-to-be college parents also believe that they will be asked for advice or assistance early and often." In a 2007 survey of future college parents, he found that 75% expected to have extreme or great concern about their children's health and safety; 66%, about finances; 62%, about academics; 55%, about career planning; and 52%, about personal relationships. About 63% of the respondents expect their children to frequently seek advice on finances; 36%, on career planning; 30%, on health and safety; 27%, on academics; and 19%, on personal relationships.

College Parents of America, which is itself another manifestation of helicopter parenting, does advocacy work at the state and federal levels on issues affecting college costs and provides its members with information about such topics as financial aid, strategies for getting into top-rated schools, and the challenges of child-parent relationships during the college years. College Parents of America clearly recognizes its role in the helicopter parent phenomenon, and in a statement to parents encourages them to forge ahead: "Helicopter pilots and the crews they carry on their missions perform important and sometimes heroic tasks. So too do helicopter parents on your mission to best support your children on the path to and through college. We wish you happy and successful piloting!" The organization even calls its blog "Hoverings."

Many parents continue to remain vigilant even beyond college, as children apply to graduate schools and enter the workplace. Hovering, it seems, can be a very hard habit to break. "We gave our kids so much, and when they got in trouble, our first instinct was to jump in and rescue them," says Donna Canavan, the mother of two millennial generation daughters in Wrentham, Massachusetts. "As they get older, we don't know how to stop giving and stop guiding." Her elder daughter moved back home after college, and Canavan is in touch almost daily with her younger daughter at Elon University in Elon, North Carolina. Canavan learned to send text messages because she knew she'd be sure to get an answer if she couldn't reach her daughters by phone. "I just need to know they're safe and happy," she says.

She believes that the competitive nature of college admissions and the workplace requires parents to be ever watchful. "Kids need to be pushed to get ahead today," she says. "You have to seek out information for them about public service internships and other opportunities." To assist her daughters, Canavan discovered some internship opportunities at the statehouse in Boston and closely monitored their college applications. "I didn't write their application essays for them," she says, "but I screamed a lot to do a good job because essays make your application pop, and they can make or break you."

THE PSYCHOLOGY OF HELICOPTER PARENTS

What makes these helicopter parents tick? Psychologists find this breed of parent both fascinating and a little disturbing. Some believe that parents don't want to let their children go partly because of their own fear of growing old. High-achieving parents also may consider their child's success a reflection on them. They want to continue the upward mobility trend in their families, so their children must do bigger and better things than they did. In essence, their children's accomplishments—even if orchestrated by the parents—increase their social status.

"In some ways, it certainly is narcissistic," says Frank Masterpasqua, a professor in the graduate clinical psychology program at Widener University in Chester, Pennsylvania. "Some parents are concerned about how it's going to reflect on them if their child doesn't get the job or isn't treated fairly. It's more than just worrying about the child." He adds, "There's almost an inability by parents to move to the next level of development and see what is their responsibility and what is their child's. But at some point, we have to realize the child should be more independent."

Masterpasqua doesn't recommend that parents suddenly cut their children off, however. "This millennial generation needs parents around longer than other generations have," he says. "It's a matter of drawing the line between what's reasonable and what's unreasonable. If they need financial support or a home temporarily to fall back on, that's fine. But parents shouldn't go out of the home and be proactive in searching for a job for their child."

College administrators fret that helicopter parents are interfering with one of the most important developments during the college years—the student's growing sense of autonomy. Even as they reach their 20s, the traditional start of independent adulthood, many millennials—dubbed "adultolescents"—are still clinging to their parents for both financial and emotional support. This delayed adulthood means that millennials may be less committed to their first few jobs. They feel more freedom to explore different careers because they have fewer responsibilities to worry about and can rely on their family for support.

CLOSE ENCOUNTERS WITH HELICOPTER PARENTS

While more companies are starting to observe helicopter parents, colleges have been seeing them most frequently and have the greatest experience in dealing with them. Given the tragic student shootings at such schools as Northern Illinois University and Virginia Polytechnic Institute and State University, parents are expected to draw even closer to their college-age children and become more vocal about campus safety.

One clear sign of the continuing close parental connection is the growth both of college parent associations and advisory councils and of offices for parent relations. Such organizations and offices didn't exist when older generations attended college, but now they're fast becoming the norm.

College parent groups give mothers and fathers a much more powerful collective voice and keep them in the know about campus developments. "You get inside information and a feel for what's really going on at a university," says Canavan, the mother from Wrentham, Massachusetts. "Your kids tell you so little and just call you a busybody." She was a member of the parent advisory council at George Washington University when her older daughter was a student there, and she hopes to become a member of the parent organization at her younger daughter's school, Elon University. "I love doing parent outreach; dealing with the parents of freshmen is like helping a new mother who just joined your baby's play group," she explains. "You get questions and issues that parents are unhappy about and can take them to the administration. Parents are so frustrated because professors won't respond when they call them and refuse to talk about grades, citing confidentiality issues."

Canavan believes that college parent organizations are teaching their children important life lessons. "They see us involved and looking for accountability," she says. "In the future, our children will come across even more strongly, challenging things and demanding responsibility and accountability."

For their part, universities have established offices for parent relations to give mothers and fathers a central place to field their questions and air their grievances. Whether separate departments or part of alumni or student affairs, they are like customer service offices to keep the consumer happy. "Many schools would prefer that parents just write a check and go away, but they realize that isn't going to happen," says Boyle, the president of College Parents of America. "With these offices, they decided it's better to feed the beast and deal with parents in a proactive way rather than have them calling the college president to ask why their son failed his geography test."

College officials at both undergraduate and graduate schools have been startled by the level of involvement of parents in their children's education. Just ask any admissions or career services director and he will tick off a list of his own close encounters with parents. Kip Harrell, associate vice president for professional and career development at the Thunderbird School of Global Management in Glendale, Arizona, sees more parents showing up at hospitality weekends for prospective M.B.A. students and asking very pointed questions about placement rates, salaries, and the companies that recruit there. "Sometimes," he says, "it's the parents asking all the questions."

Here are a couple of memorable helicopter parenting moments for Harrell. A father walked into his office, and before even introducing himself, he demanded to know, "Why haven't you found my son a job yet?" Then there was the student who called Harrell and announced, "I am conferencing my dad in on this call, as he has some questions for you."

Jeffrey Rice, head of M.B.A. career services at the Fisher College of Business at Ohio State University, was taken aback when an applicant showed up for an admissions interview with his mother in tow. Rice invited the mother to sit in on the interview, but was relieved when she declined. "The applicant told me his mother was helping him decide which school to attend," Rice says. Not all parents are willing to sit in the waiting room. A Carnegie Mellon University admissions officer spent 30 minutes with a young man and his father, but it was the father who dominated the conversation. To her amazement, the father asked how his son had done in "the interview." She hardly considered it an interview.

Millennials don't bring only parents with them. An aunt accompanied one applicant to the admissions office at the Haas School of Business at the University of California at Berkeley. He seemed delighted to have her input and told the admissions officer that she had always been intimately involved in his education.

Some college officials firmly tell pesky parents that they can deal only with the applicant and not Mom or Dad when it comes to interviews and questions about admission status. Rose Martinelli, associate dean for student recruitment and admissions at the University of Chicago Graduate School of Business, recalls receiving a call from a father demanding to know why his daughter was still on the waiting list and how she could get admitted. "I told him that his daughter needed to call me, that I couldn't discuss the matter with him," she says. "Some parents, including donors to the school, get angry when they hear that."

Why can't parents simply advise their children from home and keep their campus visits and phone calls to a minimum? That's what some college administrators wonder. But many are coming to understand that parents are so anxious and so attentive because they view themselves as investors and hold schools accountable for a proper return on their money and their children's time. As college costs have skyrocketed, parents believe they would be irresponsible if they didn't monitor their child's education. Some students and parents have even tried to demand their money back because they didn't like a certain professor or teaching assistant at Queen's University in Ontario. "We tell them we're not Wal-Mart," says Brady, the registrar.

In the Hoverings blog on the College Parents of America Web site, several people posted comments tying their close connections with their children's universities to the huge financial investment they're making. One parent wrote, "I would guess that there is a direct correlation between the time that colleges started increasing tuition and other costs at two to five times the inflation rate every year and the rising involvement level of parents. I might not expect or demand as much out of a university if it were costing me $10,000 a year as I do when it is costing me $28,000 a year. I wouldn't put $28,000 in a stock and then walk away and not pay attention to the performance of the stock."

In another posting on the blog, a parent says he has tried to back away from his college daughter but is finding it difficult. By his estimates, he will have invested $380,000 in her by the time she finishes college. "I don't mean to sound cold," he wrote, "but that's a heck of a lot of bucks out there. If for no other reason, doesn't this give me some basis to keep tabs on her progress?"

GOOD INTENTIONS

Understandably, few people are willing to identify themselves as helicopter parents—even though they fit the description to a tee. The helicopter moniker has taken on such a negative connotation that most resent the label and prefer to think of themselves as simply concerned and supportive. In fact, although some parents frequently overreact in trying to shield their children, others do try to show more restraint.

It's easy to criticize helicopter parents, but colleges and employers shouldn't be too harsh in judging them. They truly cherish their children, even if a little too much. Listening to parents who are closely bound to their children reveals that they are much more than a stereotype. Many seem to be sincere, well-intentioned folks who care deeply for their children. They argue that 18 is not a magic age when their children suddenly become fully mature and need less support from Mom and Dad.

Many parents see no harm in monitoring deadlines for tests, papers, SATs, and college applications. After all, they maintain, the homework load has mushroomed in middle schools and high schools, and it takes a bevy of extracurricular achievements to get the attention of college admissions offices. How could their children do it all if parents didn't pitch in, too?

Mercedes Rodriguez, a Cuban American physician in Orlando, Florida, conducted much of the college research for her children because they were busy enough with their studies and other high school activities. Using the Internet and guidebooks, she researched about 300 colleges and presented her son and daughter with a preliminary list of about 30 to consider. "We would have further conversations and then pare the list to about seven or eight we felt we really wanted to visit," she says. "I was very hands-on, which is probably an understatement. But my interest is that they get the best education possible."

In some ways, Rodriguez sees attentive millennial parents as a throwback to an earlier time in American society. She believes strongly in the value of a close-knit nuclear family, and she has always made it a priority for her family to eat dinner, attend church, and vacation together as often as possible. "I don't like parents who are laid back about where their kids are, given how much temptation and craziness there is today," she says. "Maybe what we've done is just go back to a more traditional way of raising a family. From the get-go, we just said to the kids that we wanted them to be a part of everything we did and that we were planning to be a big part of everything they did."

Rodriguez also has kept her children on a short leash because she believes that parents should exert their influence strongly as long as they are providing financial support. "My mom was not very involved in my schooling and didn't know half the time where I was," she says. "We, on the other hand, got very involved in the kids' schools. When my son's school started spending an inordinate amount of time teaching nonsense—ethnic days, multicultural days, and such—we pulled him out and placed him in a private school where the important subjects were reading, writing, arithmetic, history, and civics." She also offered to talk to teachers when problems arose, but her children usually preferred to handle them alone. "I have wanted to be more aggressive in sports over things that I found blatantly unfair," she says. "But they have said, 'No, Mom,' so I have held myself back and tried to cool off."

Even as her son, a student at the College of William and Mary, reached the age of 21, Rodriguez continued to review his class choices each semester. He e-mailed her a list of possible courses, and they discussed what he needed to take in order to secure a well-rounded education. In Rodriguez's opinion, that includes great literature and Greek and Roman civilization, not just the science classes he needs as a pre-med student. "The great thing is that now he requests my advice and input," she says. "It's nice."

Indeed, the good news is that millennials actually like their parents and consider them to be trusted friends. Melissa Krantz, a mother of two twentysomething daughters in Cross River, New York, says they speak with her daily, and regularly seek her advice and approval. They have sought her input on everything from college grades and activities to their dating relationships. "My daughter asked me what we thought of the guy she was dating," Krantz says, "and told us she could never think of having a relationship with someone we didn't like and approve of."

Nearly two-thirds of the 13- to 21-year-old respondents in a 2007 Harris Interactive YouthPulse survey said they would call their parents first if they were in trouble, and more than half said they trust their parents more than anyone else. When asked to name their role models, about half said their mothers, and more than a third said their fathers. Such positive feelings often carry over to other adults so that millennials tend to be congenial with their elders in the college classroom and at work, too.

Some researchers contend that the close parental ties may be beneficial to students. The 2007 National Survey of Student Engagement, which is administered by Indiana University, found that the children of helicopter parents report greater engagement, more participation in educationally useful activities, and higher satisfaction with the college experience. But students whose parents were in frequent contact and intervened often to help them solve problems in college also received lower grades. That could indicate that some parents intervened so much because their children were having academic difficulties. The survey found that 13% of first-year college students reported frequent intervention by parents, and another 25% said they intervened sometimes.

Christine Deska, a Manhattan College graduate and program assistant for AARP in New York City, is still very grateful for her parents' assistance in choosing a college and especially for seeing her through her education so that she didn't have any loans to repay after graduation. "They were extremely involved in my college decisions—as they should have been, seeing that they paid for it," she says. They helped her research college soccer teams and schools' academic records and rankings, and her mom accompanied her on visits to half a dozen campuses.

Now she remains in close contact, speaking with her parents in Maryland three or four times a week by phone. (They don't communicate more regularly by text messaging, she says, simply because her parents "can't figure it out.") But she asserts that she is quite independent today. Now, as she considers going to law school, her parents are pushing her to make her own choices. "As I look at law schools, they're much farther removed, and I'll admit it's very tough to make these decisions on my own this time around," Deska says. "Any debt I incur now is my problem, as well as paying my bills while I go to school. I can proudly say I'm completely independent, but it's not a walk in the park considering the cost of living in New York City."

BREAKING AWAY

Because some millennials have come to rely so heavily on their parents' advice, college counselors question whether they're being suffocated or supported. Helicopter parents may indeed be toxic, hampering their children's need to become self-reliant and face inevitable obstacles and disappointments in life. They may be producing a generation of very needy adults who can't think for themselves. One young woman regretfully told me, "My parents' views have become my own. I cannot claim originality when it comes to my ideas." And on an Internet blog about helicopter parents, a young man wrote, "As I got older, the struggle for independence was always there. I was always depressed, but I always put on a front to appease my parents. . . . There is a difference between being there for your children and being a helicopter parent. All of the parents out there who think they were just doing what was best for their children are fooling themselves. It's more convenient and more socially acceptable if your children are successful, but for your children to be better people, you need to know when not to help get rid of a problematic situation but to help give them support to get through it and let them know that they can do it."

Experience Inc., a Boston-based career services firm, surveyed college students and recent graduates in 2006 and found that a quarter of the respondents felt that parents were overly involved to the point that it was annoying or embarrassing. More than a third said parents had called into or attended meetings with academic advisers; 31% said parents had contacted professors to complain about a grade.

In some cases, it's a symbiotic relationship. The children want all the help—and money—they can get from their parents. Parents have even taken sabbaticals from their jobs to devote their full attention to the college application process. What's more, some college students e-mail their class assignments to their parents to edit before turning them in to their professors. In the Experience Inc. survey, about two-thirds of the respondents said they still seek counsel from parents on academic and career issues.

But some millennials crave more independence. Lindsay Ronga, a very successful millennial, wants to be more self-reliant, but knows it won't be easy. Never mind that she has reached her mid-20s and become an M.B.A. student at Harvard Business School, after having worked in the demanding fields of investment banking and private equity. Like many millennials, she still continues to consult her parents for advice even when she knows she should think for herself.

The business school application process was stressful, with tears and angry words exchanged sometimes when she consulted her parents for advice. "With every essay I wrote, I was on the phone with my father, getting his input," she recalls. "He sometimes tore my essays to shreds, and for the most part, I'd say I incorporated a moderate amount of his suggestions. It almost seemed as if he himself was applying sometimes, and I had to remind him it was me." As for her mother during the application process, "I love her to death," Ronga says, "though I got frustrated with her toward the end and politely requested that she not give me any more input." Ultimately, Ronga made her parents quite proud, gaining admission to all four of the schools she applied to.

She says she came to realize that she had worked in banking and private equity mostly to please her parents. At the time, she felt it was the right thing to do. But now she would like to move out of finance and if possible, find a career in the wine industry, her true passion. "I hope to become more independent and need less guidance and direction," she says. "But my friends and I still talk to our parents almost on a daily basis; it's just natural to us. I believe my generation loves guidance and wants to run everything—whether school, jobs, or dating—by our parents and friends."

Some parents realize that they must start backing off to avoid handicapping their children for life. They need to encourage their kids to make their own decisions and learn from the inevitable mistakes they will make. But they aren't moving into the background easily. Many parents object to what they perceive to be a move by colleges and employers to shove them aside. They argue that since preschool they have been encouraged to be partners with their children's teachers and coaches. Now everyone suddenly wants them to vanish.

"It was a mantra throughout my children's school years that parents need to be involved in their kids' lives," says Kim Foley, a Boston-area mother of two college students. "It was a badge of honor if you became a Girl Scout or Boy Scout leader, knew all the teachers' names, went to the school's parent night, and were aware that your child was reading Mark Twain this week." Then boom! "All of a sudden," she continues, "you're expected to shut it off in college. I just don't think that's right. Students want to continue the relationships that were developed over the years and need their parents' involvement in working through the big bureaucracies of large colleges."

She finds it ironic that universities ask undergraduate parents to donate to their fundraising campaigns, yet discourage them from questioning a professor's teaching style. "I'm not calling the professors, but I do want to know how their classes are going," she says. She puts her foot down, though, about some requests from her children. When her daughter was unhappy with her roommate assignment, she asked her mother to change it. "I knew I couldn't get a different roommate even if I called because the school wouldn't listen to her or to me," Foley says. "But I felt it was inappropriate to even make the call. I told my daughter that I can't always fix things."

TEDDY BEARS FOR THE EMPTY NEST

Many college officials these days pointedly tell parents at freshman orientation that it's time to start letting go. By going on the offensive, they hope to keep parents off their backs as much as possible and to let students gain more independence and self-confidence.

Colgate University in Hamilton, New York, takes a firm but very reasoned approach in its pleas to parents to help their children become more resilient, self-sufficient adults. In a welcoming message to parents on its Web site, the university calls parents "partners," but urges them to let their children learn problem-solving skills on their own. It suggests that parents ask their children questions as opposed to providing answers, encourage them to contact deans and faculty members themselves rather than make calls for them, and let them select their classes on their own. Colgate also advises parents to help their children learn to manage conflicts and negotiate differences with roommates rather than seek a quick fix by moving to another room.

At an orientation session for first-year students, Rebecca Chopp, Colgate's president, told parents, "I know it is hard to hold back, let your child solve his or her own problems, not call the school to try to fix things, but I imagine you learned to solve your own problems because others, including your parents, let you or even forced you to do so. The hope we have for the future and these young men and women is going to require that they go through difficult times and learn to survive, that they make a mistake and live with the consequences, that they transform a failure into a soaring success."

Dickinson College in Carlisle, Pennsylvania, also addresses the helicopter parent issue in a diplomatic fashion with this message: "There may be times when parental involvement is the best course of action—we're not trying to override your judgment—but for routine problems, it's best to let students handle the situations on their own. And there are trained professionals on campus to help students navigate these issues."

Dickinson even dreamed up a helicopter parent quiz. Here's a sample of the multiple-choice questions:

When visiting your student, how much do you help?

A. You don't clean his or her room. It's not your job.
B. You help to take out the trash.
C. After taking out the trash, you do the laundry.
D. You provide maid services and leave mints on the pillow.

"A" is the college's preferred answer, of course. "Maybe your GPS is programmed to take you straight to your student's residence hall or apartment, but he or she has to learn to function as an adult," the college advises.

Your student has just been found responsible for a minor conduct violation. What do you do?

A. You take a headache medication and discuss with your student the consequences of inappropriate behavior.

B. Show up on your student's doorstep.

C. Call the college president. You pay a lot of tuition. Your kid should be let off the hook.

D. Call Alan Dershowitz and print up "Free Jenny" T-shirts.

Again, "A" is the college's recommended answer. "We expect our students to behave responsibly—it's part of being an adult. Note that most violations result in minor repercussions," the college says.

Some universities try to help parents cope with their child's departure from the nest. As part of freshman orientation at Seton Hall University in South Orange, New Jersey, students and their parents assembled teddy bears together in an activity modeled after the Build-a-Bear Workshops in shopping malls. They dressed the bears in T-shirts bearing the message "Someone at Seton Hall Loves Me" and the address for the school's parent Web site. That was the gentler side of orientation.

Then they also heard from Linda Walter, an administrator who ran the orientation. She bluntly told parents, "So now that you have looked over them all these years, it's their turn to be on their own. Your job now becomes being a coach, not a cruise director." The closing slide of her presentation: "See you all at graduation!"

That's wishful thinking, of course, and Walter knows it. "Parents have been advocating for their children for years, and it isn't going to stop in college," says Walter. "What we need to do is help them understand the difference between what goes on in college and what went on in the kindergarten through high school years. They're used to calling the school principal and expect to be able to call the college president. But you can't do that."

The teddy bears are a nice touch, but parents actually need not despair when their children leave for college. It's very possible that they'll be back. Millennials are earning a reputation as "boomerang kids" who return home after college or when they quit a job. Whereas earlier generations left home for good when they moved away to college, many parents say their kids are more than welcome to come back home whenever they choose. It's a comfy safety net if they decide to drop out of college for a while, delay going to work after graduation, or quit a job they find unsatisfying.

Marva Giles, who works as an operations specialist for a bank in Atlanta, encouraged her son to return home while he looked for a job after college. "I told him not to rush, to look at a lot of different companies," she says. "He wants to get a job to pay me back for my help. But I told him there's no need to push it so fast if you've got a good relationship with your parents and can live with them for a while."

Do college graduates have any qualms about retreating to the nest? In a 2006 Life After College survey by Experience Inc., the career services firm, nearly 60% of the respondents reported moving back home after college, and about one-third remained there for more than a year. Many were motivated by financial reasons. About 59% said they felt indifferent or neutral when telling people they moved back home; 10% were proud and happy about living with Mom and Dad once again. And the other 31%? They admitted that they felt embarrassed.

CHAPTER HIGHLIGHTS

- Today's parents remain intimately involved with their millennial generation children from the cradle to the workplace.

- These so-called helicopter parents most frequently intervene during the school years, lobbying teachers for higher grades and helping their kids apply to colleges, but they also are becoming increasingly involved in the job search.

- Psychologists and educators worry that parents are making too many decisions for their children and preventing them from developing autonomy.

- Insisting that they are well intentioned, helicopter parents contend that their children need all the support they can get in the competition for admission to a top college and a rewarding job after graduation.

- Some millennials desire more independence but find it difficult to wean themselves from their parental safety net.

- Universities are telling helicopter parents that they need to let their teenagers grow up and are helping parents adjust to the empty nest.

- The nest may not be empty for long, though, because many millennials move back home after college or after a job loss.

4

Take Your Parents to Work

Employer alert: helicopter parents are whirring into the workplace. They could show up anytime, and they're butting into everything from job interviews to performance evaluations. Some are even accompanying their children to the office after they're hired.

That's what happened when Ogilvy Public Relations Worldwide in New York City invited employees' parents to spend a day at the office to get to know the firm and see just what their kids do all day to earn their paychecks. For starters, parents received a primer on PR techniques because many people mistakenly believe advertising and PR are one and the same. They also learned more about Ogilvy's own business and clients, participated in a brainstorming session, and attended a cocktail reception.

"A lot of the folks here are millennials, and we've been doing a lot of things to try to keep them happy," says Kate

Cronin, managing director of Ogilvy's New York office. "We realized that they're proud of their parents and want to share their accomplishments with them." To her surprise, more than 30 employees brought their parents to the office. "When I was their age," Cronin says, "I didn't want my parents anywhere near my job. If someone had asked me about having a parents day, I would have said, 'Are you kidding? So my father can embarrass me?'"

That certainly wasn't how Sarah Pfeiffer, an Ogilvy account supervisor, reacted. She jumped at the chance to invite her mother to come to Manhattan from Maryland and participate in Bring Your Parents to Work Day. "Overall, I thought it was really a fun way to show my mom what I do every day," she says. "PR is a field that is often confusing, so it was nice to showcase what we do here and how much fun we have doing it." It also meant a lot to Pfeiffer that Ogilvy was willing to invest the time and money to meet and socialize with parents. "I really miss being close to my family because other than a semester abroad, I have always lived within 45 minutes of home," she says. "Having my mom share a work day with me was really great."

Her mother, Carol Gallay, who works as a teacher, was equally enthusiastic, although at first she thought it was a joke. "I had had this negative image of PR people as spin doctors, but I couldn't believe my daughter would be doing that," she says. So she was eager to learn more about Sarah's job and meet her bosses and colleagues. In addition, she participated in a focus group addressing the problem of educating parents to use antibacterial ointments along with bandages for their kids' cuts and scrapes. Best of all, she ended up staying over the weekend and seeing *Mary Poppins* on Broadway with her daughter.

Some employers might think Ogilvy was asking for trouble by opening its doors willingly to parents. In fact, Ogilvy executives did feel some trepidation about how parents might behave. For one thing, they worried that parents might ask why their children don't earn more money. "I know that their parents are clearly their advisers and talk to them whenever I'm giving them a review or offering them a promotion," Cronin says. But the parents minded their manners, and Ogilvy even ended up with an ongoing panel of employees' mothers who share their thoughts on osteoporosis. (Ogilvy promotes Merck & Co.'s Fosamax as a treatment for the thinning bones disorder.)

Ogilvy was so pleased that it plans to repeat Bring Your Parents to Work Day and to expand it to offices in other cities. Given Ogilvy's success, perhaps we should establish a national Take Our Parents to Work Day, along with the traditional Take Our Daughters and Sons to Work Day every April.

Strange as it might seem to older generations, the workplace is becoming a family affair. Companies today aren't just hiring the child; they get the whole family in the bargain, like it or not. Parents are getting involved from the start of their children's careers, bugging recruiters to schedule interviews, then asking to sit in on job interviews, and even trying to negotiate salaries. The bonds are so tight that some corporate recruiters are finding that millennials prefer to work in a location near their family and friends and avoid long-term international assignments.

How pervasive is parental influence in the job search? KPMG, the global auditing firm, surveyed 2,409 U.S. business school students in 2007 and found that 17% rely on parents' guidance a great deal in choosing an employer, and nearly 40% will not accept an offer without at least speaking with their parents.

On the employer side, the Collegiate Employment Research Institute at Michigan State University conducted a survey and found that about one-third of companies with more than 3,700 workers had witnessed parental involvement in the recruiting process and the early career stages of college students. Smaller companies reported less parental activity. Employers seeking students with a business background encountered parents more often, whereas those recruiting people with engineering, computer, and scientific credentials reported the least parental involvement.

The following are the most common types of parental intervention reported in the Michigan State survey: obtaining information about a company, submitting a resume on the child's behalf, promoting the child for a job, attending a career fair, complaining if the child wasn't hired, and making interview arrangements. Some parents go even further after their child has been hired. Survey respondents said parents even complete their child's assignments to avoid missing deadlines, or review the work to improve its quality. And one respondent told of an employee who was reprimanded at work and refused to meet with or respond to the supervisor before talking with Mom and Dad.

Mothers were more likely to gather information and make arrangements for interviews and company visits; fathers were the ones who usually showed up during job and salary negotiations. Fathers also contacted companies when their child didn't land a job and when a supervisor disciplined their child. One survey respondent urged parents to at least inform their children when they have sent their resumes to an employer. "We have called a student from our resume pool," the employer said, "only to find that they did not know anything about our company and were not interested in a position with us."

Whereas Ogilvy asked parents to visit its offices, most are invading the workplace uninvited. L'Oréal's human resource managers in New York City were very surprised when parents called to investigate possible job opportunities for their children with the beauty-products company. It was something the Paris-based company hadn't experienced in its European offices.

Some employers would appreciate it if millennials would try to be more discreet about their helicopter parents. Alison Brod, president and founder of a public relations and marketing agency in New York City, simply wishes millennials wouldn't tell her they have to get Mom and Dad's blessing before taking a job. "I have offered some girls a job, and they say they have to check with their parents first," Brod says. "It's fine if they want to get the advice, but please don't tell me that when you're 21 years old. I always believed that 21 meant I was a grown-up who was expected to make decisions on my own and would have never ever shared that with a prospective employer—even though I too needed to speak to my parents."

Some parents even encourage unethical behavior. The parents of a University of Texas M.B.A. student urged her to renege on a job offer she had already accepted because they thought more highly of another company that also wanted to hire her. "She eventually decided not to do this after talking with our staff," says Stacey Rudnick, director of M.B.A. career services at Texas's McCombs School of Business in Austin. "But she continually asserted that she needed to 'look after her own best interests' when we discussed it. Despite the fact that the second company was not as closely aligned to her long-term career interests as the first one, the weight of its brand name made her parents think she was making a bad decision."

Some frustrated supervisors find that their new hires are so bound to their parents that they consult them about day-to-day work decisions. They might announce that they're on board with a decision because Mom thinks it's a splendid idea or try to wiggle out of a work commitment because the timing isn't good for Mom.

Lorrie Foster, executive director of councils and research working groups at the Conference Board, a business research organization in New York City, was startled when she first encountered parental intervention in a workplace decision. An employee decided that she wasn't going to travel to a business meeting, but hadn't bothered to inform anyone. "When I asked the young woman what was going on, she said she couldn't talk right then but would get back to me," Foster recalls. "When she did a few moments later, she said that her mother says she shouldn't have to travel to the meeting because her family might be doing something the day after she got back from the trip." Unsure she had heard the woman correctly, Foster probed further to determine whether the reasoning for her decision was really coming from her mother. "She said yes, and repeated the response without the least bit of embarrassment," Foster says.

Even performance reviews aren't off-limits. The head of a small advertising agency tells of a friend who was flabbergasted when an employee's father showed up the day of his son's very first performance review. What proved even more amazing was the employee's failure to grasp why the review wouldn't take place with the father in attendance. If performance reviews sound harsh or pay raises seem stingy, employers had better watch out. Just as they complained to teachers and principals about unacceptable grades, some parents are now calling managers to object to the size of pay increases and to performance evaluations that fall short of being rave reviews.

Although there's no question that millennial parents will be a fact of life for employers, companies are taking a wide variety of approaches in dealing with mothers and fathers. Some are very disturbed by what they consider totally inappropriate behavior and would like to banish parents from the workplace. To them, parents represent a growing occupational hazard that must be stopped now.

But if they are too intolerant, they are likely to offend their young prospects and could eventually lose them to another employer. A far better strategy is to devise ways to involve parents without letting them become too intrusive. Whatever approach they take, companies cannot wish these persistent parents away, no matter how much they'd like to. Parents aren't going to suddenly stop working for their children's success after more than two decades of such a close attachment.

"It's going to be a real challenge for companies to define the boundaries in this relationship," says Daphne Atkinson, a consultant on business schools and management education. "But they don't have to take a judgmental position; they can take a more pragmatic approach. Parents are trusted advisers of their children, so companies need to work productively with them, while taking into account that certain employee information is confidential."

SETTING LIMITS—ON THE PARENTS

To be sure, companies absolutely must set limits. But establishing the ground rules requires some finesse to avoid alienating millennial employees and their parents. It's best to take a positive approach, emphasizing the need for Junior to become more independent to prosper in his new career. Companies also may have to point out their established human resource procedures so that parents understand that denying them access to private personnel information is nothing personal. It's just standard corporate policy.

For their part, parents certainly should demonstrate greater restraint and discretion in the workplace. They need to remind themselves that they aren't their child's personal agent, representing their darling as if she were a star athlete or entertainer. How far parents can go will depend partly on how much a prospective employer wants their child. But regardless of how aggressively a company might court their son or daughter, parents should use common sense and not make ridiculous demands. They definitely should avoid getting directly involved in employment interviews and negotiations, not only because it's highly inappropriate but also because they could end up killing a possible job offer. Recruiters will certainly get ticked off, and the parents' tactics may reflect negatively on their children. Employers may believe that the young people lack initiative, decisiveness, and the ability to think for themselves—which may well be the case.

Parents should understand that employers are far different from educators. Parents can't bully companies the way they did schools. Through their taxes and tuition, they had a bigger personal stake in schools and colleges. But if parents expect to play a similar role in the workplace, they will only succeed in embarrassing their children and straining the relationship with the employer. If a parent contacts a child's supervisor to criticize the workload or compensation, the child may never regain the boss's respect and support.

Generally, parents will find that companies are adamant about making job interviews and questions about work responsibilities and performance reviews off-limits to family members. International Business Machines Corp. has permitted parents to attend student receptions to learn more about the company, but otherwise it prefers to deal only with the applicants. "We want parents to be comfortable, but we try to stress that there's an appropriate balance we need to strike," says Julie Baskin Brooks, Americas staffing leader for IBM. "If parents call us, we tell them that we appreciate their support, but would prefer to have conversations with their son or daughter. It's a matter of confidentiality."

Some pushy parents can't seem to control themselves and can become downright obnoxious with recruiters. Natalie Griffith, manager of human resource programs at Eaton Corp., an industrial manufacturer, gets calls from parents trying to arrange job interviews for their children. When she tells them the child must set it up himself, some parents get testy, accusing her of not working with them and threatening to call her supervisor. She says she tells parents, "You have to realize that your child will be on his own soon and will have to do things for himself. He needs to take the steps himself to get information about Eaton and ask for an interview."

Steve Canale, recruiting manager at General Electric Co., has received calls from brazen parents attempting to negotiate higher compensation or complaining that their child didn't hear back from the company after her interview. GE doesn't give into parents' demands, but it also doesn't hold their behavior against the prospective employee. "Sometimes kids have absolutely no control over their parents," Canale says. "But we make it clear to parents that we will deal only with their child." He believes helicopter parenting intensified after the terrorist attacks of September 11, 2001, as mothers and fathers worried more about safety issues when their children moved to new cities to take jobs.

Perhaps most outrageous are the parents who not only insist on sitting in on their child's job interview but also ask the company to pay for their transportation to its offices. Hard to believe? Well, that has actually happened to recruiters at FedEx Corp. The company doesn't cover parents' expenses, of course, and it also doesn't permit family members in the interview room. But it does let them tour its offices. "Most of our managers are welcoming to parents," says John Leech, FedEx's director of recruitment, "but some complain that we're not hiring the family. I gently remind them that 'Yes, we are hiring the family.' In fact, we want to hire the students' entire tribe of friends and family. We want to become part of their personal network, which has a lot more influence in attracting future talented employees than any recruiting ad."

Millennials may discourage their parents from meddling in their jobs but still find themselves in embarrassing situations. Dan Black, director of Americas campus recruiting at Ernst & Young, recalls a particularly obnoxious call from a summer intern's parents during a company conference in Florida. They were worried about their daughter because she hadn't called them the night before and held the accounting firm responsible. They demanded to know "what kind of program we were running," Black recalls. "When we found their daughter and told her who was on the phone, she was mortified and broke into tears. I would say that they were uber-involved parents."

Some parental involvement is irritating but relatively harmless. For example, parents call Goldman Sachs Group Inc. to ask which college their child should attend to have a better shot at joining the investment banking firm. Goldman recruiters also say that more parents are pressuring employees they know at the firm to recommend their children for jobs.

Some parents may keep a lower profile and influence their children's career decisions from the sidelines. But companies can still clearly sense their presence. When they hear questions from students about 401K plans and other benefits that many young people don't usually ask much about, they figure that Mom and Dad are actively involved. In fact, Ernst & Young has begun including more information about retirement plans and other benefits in its job-offer packages because it expects parents to scrutinize every detail. It also puts information about job opportunities at the firm on a computer memory stick and tells students they can pass it along to parents when they ask how the job search is going.

Patty Phillips, executive director of career management at the Simon Graduate School of Business at the University of

Rochester, believes that school career services offices and companies can minimize the stress if they learn to anticipate parents' questions and objections. She knows that she could coach a student on the ideal career path without making much headway until Mom and Dad think it's a swell idea, too. "You have to arm yourself by giving students reasons for the advice that they can later repeat to Mom or Dad," Phillips says.

Occasionally, parents call the Simon School worried that their children are messing up salary and benefit negotiations with employers. "In such cases, we have to worry about confidentiality and can't share specifics," Phillips says, "but we can give the salary range our graduates in investment banking received last year or the average signing bonuses given to those who went into brand management."

REACHING OUT TO PARENTS

A small but growing number of companies are trying to woo parents, as well as their children, for a very simple and selfish reason: they hope that enlisting parents as their allies will help them attract and retain millennials. Companies realize that parents are often pulling the strings in their children's job search, pushing them to pursue certain careers. Consequently, to land a strong job candidate who is weighing two employment offers, companies sometimes try to assuage parents' fears and uncertainty. A senior executive at a financial services firm, for instance, decided to call a promising applicant's mother because she had told her daughter that the banking industry was unstable. He failed to change the mother's mind, however, and the daughter ended up taking a management consulting job instead.

Perhaps the most accommodating employer these days is Enterprise Rent-A-Car. Unlike many employers, it doesn't view interacting with parents in a negative light at all. Enterprise's attitude is that it's best to provide complete and accurate information about the company and job offers to parents because millennials will most likely want to consult them and capitalize on their knowledge and experience.

If job candidates ask that their parents be part of the hiring process, Enterprise readily includes them. It mails parents "welcome letters" from vice presidents, and information packets about the company, job opportunities, and employee benefits. Most striking is Enterprise's willingness to let parents listen in on the telephone when the company offers a job to their children. Parents are supposed to abide by the ground rules and not make any comments on the phone. Later, after discussing the offer and the compensation package with their children, they can call Enterprise recruiters back and pose questions.

"We welcome the fact that parents want to help their children make decisions," says Marie Artim, assistant vice president for recruiting at Enterprise. "We want to make them feel more comfortable about a company they may not know well before their child decides to join us."

Most companies don't let parents get nearly as involved as Enterprise does. Indeed, some recruiting managers laugh in disbelief when they hear that parents can become such active participants in job offers. A few employers, however, are considering following Enterprise's lead, but only to a point. They say they might be amenable to providing job descriptions and benefit information in writing to parents, but they want to limit the conversations and meetings to the job candidate.

Meanwhile, some companies have used their Web sites to communicate with parents. For instance, Office Depot Inc. included a parents section on its careers Web site with an empathic message: "You may be anticipating your child's graduation with mixed emotions: You are proud of what your child has accomplished so far, but probably melancholic about your 'baby' moving on to his or her next step and concerned about them being able to provide for themselves. . . . Many parents want to be involved and supportive of their child's career without being too involved."

Similarly, the U.S. Army recruiting Web site addresses parents' concerns about their children enlisting during wartime and touts the benefits of college financial aid and leadership training. Given the potential dangers that soldiers face, the Army understandably feels both an obligation and an urgent need to begin a dialogue with parents. "This generation listens more to their parents and seeks their affirmation," says Lt. Col. Shawn Buck, chief of the market research and analysis division of the U.S. Army Accessions Command. When he was a university professor of military science, he recalls that some parents were very vocal about their opposition to the armed forces, sometimes even offering their children gifts if they didn't enlist. "I remember one father offered his son half of his business to keep him out of the military," Buck says.

Mothers, however, are the biggest challenge. The Army's research found that only about a quarter of mothers are likely to recommend military service, compared with 33% of fathers and 41% of grandparents. Moms also are the most likely to try to talk their children out of joining the armed forces, but they also are the least knowledgeable about the military. Given that lack of information, the Army hopes to influence both mothers and fathers through its Web site.

When mothers and fathers click on the parents section of the site, they immediately get this pitch: "You made them strong. We'll make them Army strong." They can download a "discussion tool kit," in which the Army urges parents to let their children pursue their dreams: "Your son or daughter may still be your little baby, but don't treat him or her like one. It takes a lot of courage to even consider the Army. Respect that." There are also features describing daily life at an Army post, deployment to Iraq or Afghanistan, and ways to keep in touch by telephone, mail, the Internet, and personal visits.

Probably the most influential parts of the Web site are the testimonials from families discussing the hard decision of letting children become soldiers. In one video, Molly Anderson talks about her daughter Sgt. Autumn Anderson and how Autumn's announcement about joining the Army Reserve shocked her. As a single mother, Molly says, she had a "protective mother bear instinct," but "eventually, I did see it Autumn's way. I had no choice but to allow her to create her own world."

Millennial parents arouse sympathy in some employers. They understand that most parents don't mean any harm and are just looking out for their children's happiness and security. Matthew Schuyler, for one, strongly believes in tactful diplomacy with parents. As chief human resources officer for Capital One Financial Corp., he observes plenty of helicopter parents but isn't offended by them. Parents want to see the offices where their kids are going to work, and they pepper the human resources department with questions about job offers. Recruiters for the financial services company politely answer their questions and correspond with them, mailing out the corporate annual report and brochures. "Talking to parents is a good thing because there's something to be leveraged here," Schuyler believes. "If we call a student at home during a school break and get the parent on the line, we take full advantage of that to tell them how great their child is and how much we want him or her at Capital One. It's no different from sports teams involving parents when they recruit a player."

On campus, a few parents have tried to crash the job interview, which puts Capital One recruiters in a delicate situation. They don't want to upset the parents, so they turn on the charm in the waiting room and try to divert their attention away from the interview. "Our recruiters become sort of armchair psychiatrists" to gently rein parents in, Schuyler says. "In some ways, these parents are living vicariously, and in some ways, they want to prevent their children from making the same mistakes they did when they started their careers."

Like Capital One, Northwestern Mutual Life Insurance Co. sees parents as partners in helping recruit their children. For example, it invites parents of some of its top-performing interns to attend its annual meeting in Milwaukee. Former intern Mark Kull took his parents to the meeting and believes that the experience really sold them on Northwestern Mutual and his plans to pursue a career as a financial representative. "They sat there with Northwestern's financial advisers listening to the speeches and realized this is a real career, not just peddling insurance products," Kull says. "I already felt passionately about Northwestern, but it never hurts to have the family's support."

Now as a Northwestern Mutual financial representative in Louisville, Kentucky, Kull reaches out to the parents of his office's interns. "We invite their parents to spend an evening at the office," he says, "and when an intern does something good, I'll send a handwritten note to parents. I tell them we're proud of their child and give them my cell phone number to call if they have any questions."

Official parent days like the one at Ogilvy are likely to become more commonplace. They may prove especially beneficial for parents of younger college students taking summer internships with companies. A notable example is Merrill Lynch & Co., which invited parents of some of its summer interns to its New York City headquarters to see where their children would be working and take a look at the Wall Street area of Manhattan. Parents toured the brokerage firm's equities trading floor, learned about investment banking, heard presentations from Merrill executives and managers about career opportunities, and met some of the people their children would be working with. The goal was to ingratiate the firm with parents and overcome any reservations they might have about their children spending their summer with such a big company in such a big city.

Companies have received some criticism for encouraging helicopter parenting with such events, but Merrill defends its parent day as a well-intentioned response to millennials' desire to involve their families in their careers. "Sometimes you feel like an enabler for the parents," says a manager at Merrill, "but we decided to roll with the helicopter parent issue rather than try to fight it."

Merrill sees its parent day as giving it a strategic edge in the intense competition among banks for top college graduates. It hopes the good will it creates will help convert summer interns into full-time hires after graduation. Indeed, many parents came away with peace of mind and the sense that

Merrill cares about its employees and not just the bottom line. Toni and Leonard Simon of Houston, Texas, believe that the parent day played a significant role in their daughter Tonyel's decision to accept a full-time offer from Merrill. "Because Merrill Lynch showed so much interest in her family, she knew their values were in line with hers," Toni Simon says. "Tonyel had offers from other banks, but none offered the opportunity for parents to visit." The Simons rode the city subways to get a feel for their daughter's commute to work, visited the World Trade Center site of the terrorist attacks, and dined in restaurants near Merrill's offices. "It was a very informative and reassuring experience," says Toni Simon.

Rena Arbuthnot of Shreveport, Louisiana, was also impressed when she attended Merrill's parent day with her son. She notes that she particularly liked the "Wall Street finance 101 workshop that was offered so that we wouldn't be confused by the lingo he'd be using." Before the visit, she had perceived Wall Street firms to be cutthroat and "not the best environment" for her son. "But the visit to Merrill Lynch really put my mind at ease," she says. "The people I met seemed warm and concerned about the interns." Given such reactions, Merrill deemed the parent event a resounding success and has made it an annual affair.

Goldman Sachs, a Merrill competitor, has considered a parent event in the United States, but hasn't organized anything yet. However, it does invite both parents and students interested in a career in operations to its Spend a Day@GS event in India. They have lunch, tour the office, and meet with senior leaders.

Goldman takes pains to deal with parents' hesitation about their children joining India's outsourcing industry. Parents often believe that outsourcing jobs are low-end and monotonous, with little chance for career advancement. But Goldman tells parents that GS India is not an outsourced office but rather an integral part of the company and that their children could eventually advance to associate or vice president positions. The company also tries to allay parents' worries about the safety of their children, especially women, who might end up working the night shift. It guarantees that employees on late shifts will be picked up and dropped off at their homes. Based on job acceptance rates of 75% to 80%, Goldman says it believes that the event helps cement its relationship with the students and parents.

Still, some companies question whether millennials really want them to reach out directly to parents. Harris Corp., a communications and information technology company, surveyed engineering students and discovered that they preferred that the company not include a FAQ section for parents on its careers Web site and not send letters and other information to their parents. "We know that parents are involved because we see a lot of job acceptances after a school break when the students have gone home and discussed the offers with their parents," says Cindy Kane, director of corporate relations at Harris. "But I think some students don't want us to reach out directly to parents because they want to believe they're more independent."

A HELICOPTER MISSION FAILURE

Many companies wish helicopter parents had become more involved in one workplace issue: how to behave in the office and at social events. Remember Mom's lectures about standing up straight, using the proper fork, eating slowly—and with your mouth shut? Well, a lot of millennials don't seem to have received such pointers.

Ironically, helicopter parents haven't been vigilant enough when it comes to practical but important life lessons. In their zeal to instill self-esteem and heap on the praise, they have neglected to teach millennials some of the basic etiquette rules that could give them polish and help advance their careers—such as keeping iPods and cell phones turned off during meetings and, oh yes, showing up for work on time.

Now colleges, business schools, and employers are trying to make up for parents' failure to teach their kids proper workplace and social etiquette. During orientation for new employees, some employers must tell millennials that it's rude to answer their cell phones when they're with clients or customers.

Gretchen Neels, a Boston-based consultant, has seen or heard it all in her experience teaching etiquette to business school students and young law firm associates. Get her going and she'll tell you about the law firm associate who went to lunch with a partner and ordered the salade niçoise, pronouncing it "ni-cozy." He proceeded to gobble down much of it—green beans, boiled eggs, and olives—with his hands. Then she'll tell about the time a law firm asked her to help prepare 30 new associates for a black-tie event. She had to field such questions as, "Do I have to wear a tie?" and "What's with all the forks and glasses on the table?"

Where were the helicopter parents for these uncouth millennials? Neels traces it back to their unwillingness to act like a parent when it came to dishing out discipline or criticism. "Their attitude was let's all be pals and have a nice time," she says. "If they tried to correct their kids for eating with their mouths open and holding their forks the wrong way, the kids told them they were being mean and critical. So the parents just said, 'You know what? Eat any way you want.'"

CHAPTER HIGHLIGHTS

- Helicopter parents have invaded the workplace—contacting recruiters, asking to sit in on their children's job interviews, and even trying to negotiate salaries.

- After landing a job, some millennials still consult parents about day-to-day work issues and invite them to performance reviews with the boss.

- Savvy companies are trying to accommodate parents to some degree; the trick is to establish proper boundaries without offending prospective young employees and their parents.

- The best approach may be to establish an arm's-length relationship with parents, mailing them information about their children's job offers and allowing them to visit company offices. Interviews and performance reviews should definitely be off-limits.

- To help recruit and retain millennials, a few employers are creating official parent days, inviting parents to spend an entire day at the office to get to know the company better.

- Companies should be prepared to deal with one significant failing of helicopter parents: neglecting to teach their children proper workplace and social etiquette.

5

How Am I Doing?

For Catherine Solazzo, there is nothing quite like the sweet sound of "This was a job well done." A fabulous performance review at work is the ultimate reward for the marketing program manager at International Business Machines Corp.

"Money is always important, don't get me wrong," she says, "but for me, a high performance rating means more than a check. Nothing makes you want to dedicate yourself to a job more than recognition for the work you do." She hates unpleasant surprises, so she makes sure that she not only receives a midyear review but also meets with her managers one-on-one weekly to monitor her performance.

Like many other achievement-oriented millennials, Solazzo values feedback so much because she saw its benefits as she grew up. "I was very involved in music and competed at a national level," she says, "so the feedback of my coaches and parents was how I learned where improvements needed to be made or where praise was given."

Even at IBM, she can still elicit particularly valuable feedback from her parents and please them with high performance ratings. Her parents also happen to work at IBM and understand the magnitude of a promotion or other recognition. "When I have been promoted or have received awards, it is more special because my parents can identify with my success on a more personal level," she explains. She has indeed given her parents reason to beam, with two promotions and three awards in three years.

Besides positive reviews from her managers, Solazzo also relishes IBM "Thanks!" awards from her peers for going above and beyond her normal responsibilities. They entitle her to a small gift, but more rewarding is the personalized note she and her manager receive explaining her contributions. "I love receiving that note from my peers in my inbox saying I have been recognized and knowing my manager has been made aware of how I have helped," she says. "I believe our generation craves recognition; it helps us become more motivated and productive."

It used to be that no news was good news in the workplace. That, at least, was the perspective of older generations, who figured that silence from their superiors meant they were doing their jobs well enough. But like Solazzo, many millennials expect regular updates on their performance and thrive on positive reinforcement. For millennials, the more feedback the better. An annual or even semiannual evaluation isn't nearly enough for most millennials. They want to know how they're doing weekly, even daily. Just as they can continuously see their scores and levels when they play video games, so they also want to keep a close watch on their ratings in the workplace.

Millennials can't tolerate silence. If they don't get fast feedback on their work, some will impatiently start e-mailing or text messaging their managers. If that doesn't generate a reaction, they try hunting bosses down. Some anxious millennials consider no response equivalent to a negative response.

"There's a bit of gluttony about wanting feedback," says Subha Barry, managing director and head of global diversity and inclusion at Merrill Lynch & Co. "The millennials were raised with so much affirmation and positive reinforcement that they come into the workplace needy for more."

Millennials contend that positive feedback builds their confidence and makes them feel more secure. It provides validation that their careers are on the fast track and helps them figure out how they can improve and advance even more quickly. "I feel very competitive," says Solazzo. "I always want to know that I'm moving toward a promotion."

In addition to more frequent and detailed performance assessments, millennials want companies to nurture their career development. They are clamoring for more coaching, training, and mentoring programs. After making job offers to college graduates, some recruiters are surprised when students immediately ask how often their company does performance reviews and whether they provide mentors.

What employers are feeling are the effects of all the praise lavished on millennials as children and teenagers. Although millennials like working in teams and sharing the workload and credit, they are still hungry for individual recognition, too. Their need for applause knows no bounds. Managers claim that some millennials are such praise junkies that they want to be complimented just for showing up at work and for simply completing an assignment on time, regardless of the quality of the work.

"This generation's sense of entitlement to feedback is mind blowing," says Deborah Holmes, director of corporate social responsibility at Ernst & Young. When she was a junior employee, she could tell what her manager thought of her memos just by the number of changes that were made to them. Now, she says, millennials want to sit down and discuss their manager's opinion of the memo in detail. "It can make a supervisor feel overwhelmed," she says. "But I am impressed by this generation's understanding of the value of regular feedback in calibrating their performance." In recruiting students, the accounting firm makes sure that it promotes its "feedback-rich environment" and promises them ongoing access to "peer counselors," as well as trained career counselors.

Ernst & Young enjoys a bit of an edge. Many millennials especially like consulting, accounting, and other professional services firms because they usually provide a thorough performance evaluation after each project. To compete more aggressively for millennials, companies in other industries also are moving to semiannual or even more frequent feedback, both formal and informal. Diana Bing, director of learning at IBM, encourages managers to provide as many appraisals as possible to help employees hone their skills and become more aware of their strengths and foibles. "We suggest to managers that at the very least, they do reviews a couple of times a year on performance and career development, and preferably even more," she says. "I believe millennials demand reviews not because they need stroking, but because they value their own marketability and want someone to honestly tell them what they need to do better."

To help retain talent, L'Oréal now provides employees with formal feedback twice a year through its talent development program. They learn not only about their immediate performance but also about their major assets and long-term growth opportunities. The assessment program lets employees know what potential the beauty-products maker sees for them in the next three to five years and which skills they must cultivate if they aspire, for example, to be a manager in Latin America.

The Conference Board, a business research organization based in New York City, also has decided to provide employees with two written evaluations a year. "We've found that our twentysomething administrators want feedback on a very regular basis," says Lorrie Foster, executive director of councils and research working groups. "They also want to know where they can go next. I recently hired a talent management expert to give them a lot of attention. He takes them out for coffee and lunch, and we have set up the mechanism to give them at least monthly informal feedback."

The Conference Board also has observed how much millennials crave promotions and other rewards. "We found that this group of employees likes to work in a collaborative fashion," Foster says, "so we put them into three teams. For each team, we appointed a lead. That gave our three hardest-working administrators a promotion and gives the rest something to aspire to." If promotions to higher management levels aren't readily available, companies may need to find opportunities for lateral growth in other business units or other countries in order to keep millennials engaged.

Some employers admire millennials for their persistence in seeking instructive feedback. Carol Calkins, a partner at

PricewaterhouseCoopers, sees the demand for "instant feed-back" both at her firm and at colleges where she interacts with students. When she helps judge accounting competitions at business schools, she says, the losing teams "want a lot of feed-back about what the winning team did right and what they could have done better. They are very intense and competi-tive and want to learn from the feedback."

Similarly, during the recruiting process, some millennial students who don't get hired feel compelled to know why they didn't make the cut. Career services directors say millennials badger them, demanding to get in touch with recruiters to learn why they didn't get invited for a second-round interview. When the directors explain that companies are likely to give a "vanilla" answer that isn't very revealing, the students ask the school to contact the recruiters on their behalf for more honest reactions.

SINGING THEIR PRAISES

How did millennials become so hungry for feedback and praise? It started the day they were born, when parents and other relatives began bragging about how special they were and celebrating every milestone of their lives. Taking their first steps and speaking their first words were major accom-plishments, worthy of kudos and presents. Then there were the graduation ceremonies and gifts when the millennials moved from preschool to kindergarten. By the time they hit first grade, it's no wonder that they felt like the center of the universe.

Millennials heard the words "Good job" just for swinging a bat or finishing homework. In sports, everyone received trophies and medals, whether he sat out the season on the bench or hit home runs as the team's most valuable player. When their children didn't receive sports trophies, parents bought their own for their disappointed darlings, sometimes fibbing and claiming they were actually from the coach. One mother even told me that her daughter asked if she would receive a prize when she had her first menstrual period. Surprised but touched, her mother kindly told her, "No, but this does mean you have a new responsibility."

The craving for recognition in the workplace is also understandable, given the millennial generation's intense focus on school grades and test scores. As federal and state agencies required annual achievement tests from elementary school through high school, millennials became accustomed to receiving a regular assessment of how they stacked up against their fellow students and other students throughout the state.

Concerned about attaining a superlative grade-point average for college applications, many millennials—and their parents—have become particularly obsessed with grades in high school. Millennials want to track their progress weekly, even daily. A troubling development is the constant online access to grades in many school districts. For example, some Internet sites allow parents and their children 24/7 access to every grade in every class. When a teacher enters a grade in the system, the student's average for the quarter is automatically recalculated. Such a system surely feeds the obsession with grades.

Once they're in college, millennials continue to concentrate on making the grade. Professors note that students grow anxious if they don't receive grades regularly throughout their courses and seem much more concerned about the final grade than about what they have learned. "Our students focus so much on grades because it's so hard to get into a place like Dartmouth," says Faith Beasley, associate professor of French at Dartmouth College in Hanover, New Hampshire. "Once they get in, they'll even shy away from professors who are known as tough graders." Beasley knows that all too well. Despite her reputation as an outstanding teacher, her strict grading policy sometimes results in smaller enrollments. "When you get an A in my class, it's an A you can be really proud of," she tells students. But when reality hits, students are sometimes shell-shocked. One student told her that her father didn't pay Dartmouth's high tuition so she could receive a mere B in French.

"There are some students who want constructive criticism, but the vast majority think they know everything and really just want positive feedback," Beasley says. Once a student gave Beasley a stamp with a smiley face on it. "You don't say anything nice; you only critique us," the young woman told Beasley. "So use this stamp when you think something is good."

The millennials' need for acclaim in the workplace has also been fueled by a number of cultural factors—from children's television programs like *Mister Rogers' Neighborhood* with their message that everybody's special to the self-esteem movement that blossomed in the 1980s. California officials even created a government task force to promote self-esteem. More recently in England, there was an unsuccessful push to ban the word "failure" from schools and replace it with the term "deferred success."

Some educators warn that too little criticism and too much unwarranted praise could actually encourage complacency and make millennials less willing to take the risks necessary to truly excel. Over time, too much praise for too many people could even make the adulation seem rather meaningless. There's a telling moment in the popular animated movie *The Incredibles*, when the superhero mother tells her son that "Everyone's special," and he replies, "Which is another way of saying no one is."

Some researchers believe that all the ego massaging has clearly made the millennial generation more narcissistic. "Young people born after 1982 are the most narcissistic generation in recent history," declares Jean Twenge, a psychology professor at San Diego State University, who along with other researchers analyzed the responses of college students to the Narcissistic Personality Inventory between 1982 and 2006. On the inventory, students respond to such statements as "If I ruled the world, it would be a better place" and "I think I am a special person." The professors found that 30% more students showed elevated levels of narcissism in 2006, compared to 1982.

"I think we have been creating a softer generation, not a greater generation," says Karen Boroff, dean of the Stillman School of Business at Seton Hall University. "The 2Rs that we haven't been teaching enough are resourcefulness and resilience. Young people have been told they're so great, but now they don't have the antibodies for dealing with criticism and failure."

HANDLE WITH CARE

Millennials' need for recognition clearly brings new challenges for companies. Some employers consider millennials self-indulgent and high maintenance and are resisting demands for regular status reports on their performance. Managers say they have plenty of thoughts about their young employees' pros and cons, but can't spare the time to give feedback after every meeting and assignment.

Other companies, however, are realizing they need to be a bit more patient and understanding because they can't undo more than 20 years of being conditioned to receive praise. Rather than view it as coddling, some companies believe that regular feedback, including some well-deserved pats on the back, can be beneficial to the company as well as to this ambitious generation. They see the potential for eliciting the best from their millennial employees if they can persuade supervisors to be more cognizant of the need for frequent feedback and can establish more continuous performance evaluation and reward programs. But unlike parents and coaches, employers understand that they should reward tangible achievement, not the millennials' mere presence and participation in the workplace. Meting out praise when it's truly justified will prove to be not only more meaningful but also more motivating.

Some companies see value in small acts of kindness. At Northwestern Mutual Life Insurance Co., even very busy managers fire off congratulatory e-mail messages when young financial representatives return from a fruitful sales call, telling them "Good job!" Those particular words may be quite effective because they're reminiscent of childhood praise from parents and coaches. "We can't always sit down right away to satisfy the millennial generation's expectation of immediate response and support, but an e-mail is an easy way of communicating quickly," says Michael Van Grinsven, director of Northwestern Mutual's internship program, which recruits an average of 2,000 interns each year. "They are conditioned to getting quick feedback; they just want to know that you've heard them."

Millennials will likely take constructive suggestions for improvement to heart because they're eager to please bosses just as they did their parents and teachers. To retain a valued employee, however, managers must tread lightly when making a critique. They are finding that some millennials don't respond well to criticism and failure. If something goes awry and they are reprimanded, millennials conclude that the boss doesn't respect them, and they become extremely frustrated. A withering look or sarcastic comment can devastate them. Remember that this generation was treated so delicately that many schoolteachers stopped grading papers and tests in harsh-looking red ink.

Some managers have seen millennials break down in tears after a negative performance review and even quit their jobs in the middle of the day without notice. The owner of a public relations agency tells of a young woman who "tearfully resigned because she said that she had been a superstar at all of her other companies, but at my company, she was not."

"They like the constant positive reinforcement, but don't always take suggestions for improvement well," says Steve Canale, recruiting manager at General Electric Co. "Constructive criticism is hard for some because as children they got so much positive feedback. So now, when we do the performance evaluation, managers have changed their approach a bit. It's still important to give the good, the bad, and the ugly, but with a more positive emphasis."

Northwestern Mutual tries to soften the blow when millennials have a bad day. "We have to keep in mind that our interns are on the front lines making sales calls to prospects and that we need to respond to their emotional need for support and feedback," Van Grinsven says. He sees an unsuccessful sales call as an opportunity to motivate rather than criticize a young Northwestern Mutual employee. "We would tell someone who had a bad appointment with a potential customer that he is one appointment closer to success, even though things didn't go the way he wanted," Van Grinsven says. "When they fail, we have to ask them what they've learned and how they can prepare for the next time they fail. They have to start to understand that when they feel they're failing, they're really on the road to success."

Kanika Raney, campus recruiting chief for the financial services company Wachovia Corp., supervises a team of about a dozen millennials and has learned to take a milder approach, too. "I'm a very direct person, but I try to be careful when coaching these young people because I see that it can be detrimental," she says. "They're such go-getters who have always succeeded, so they feel like their world's falling apart if they get any criticism." For one thing, she always makes a point of giving a balanced critique that highlights her employees' most positive attributes as well as their weak spots.

When one of her team members showed poor people skills by talking down to some colleagues or speaking only to those she liked, Raney called her in for a consultation. "I told her that she wasn't always a great leader, and she cried," Raney says. "But I also pointed out her strengths as an individual contributor to try to make it less painful for her."

Of course, not all millennials are delicate flowers. Some say they can take whatever their managers dish out. "Bring it on," declares Lena Licata, a millennial and a senior member of the technology and information services practice at Ernst & Young. "It's nice to know you're doing something right and that your efforts are appreciated. But I have to know right away if I need to improve because I'm definitely not okay with not being on top. For some reason, when it comes to larger goals, I have succeeded best when I'm told I can't achieve something. It gives me the motivation to prove myself."

Whether the reviews are glowing or not, she does expect regular feedback both at work and play. For the past 17 years, she has become used to constant feedback during her horseback riding lessons: "shoulders back" and "fix your hands." "Each criticism I receive improves my riding," she says, "so I see the value in constant feedback." At Ernst & Young, Licata "loves it" that she receives a performance evaluation every few months after completing a project. Twice a year, those reviews are compiled into summary assessments that she discusses with her counselor and management team. At one of those meetings, she receives a rating that determines her raise.

But even all those reviews aren't enough to satisfy her appetite for feedback. She also asks for more frequent informal status reports on her progress. "I try to set touch-point meetings with my senior managers to discuss where they think I can improve," she says. "I find this extremely helpful for my development, as well as reducing surprises in my reviews at work."

MENTORING THE MILLENNIALS

Along with continuous feedback on how they're doing, millennials want to know what the payoff is for a praiseworthy performance. They expect companies to tell them how they can develop their skills to enhance their performance and move up in the organization. They want a career compass that shows them where their best opportunities lie and how they can reach them. That means extensive mentoring, coaching, and training programs to help them meet their goals.

"This generation would like to know as specifically as possible what their progress at the company will be," says Canale, the General Electric recruiting manager. "That's hard in any company, but especially in a company as big as GE with so many businesses and potential opportunities. But we are trying to articulate career progress more clearly because it's a selling point. For recruiting purposes, we're creating profiles of people and where they are two, four, or five years after they come out of our leadership development programs."

When KPMG surveyed college business students in 2007 and asked them to identify their primary consideration in picking an employer, more than half cited career opportunities, far more than the 12% naming salary and benefits. "The millennial generation clearly wants feedback from us, so we have an open-door policy that means they can feel free to walk into a partner's office and talk about their career progress," says Manny Fernandez, the accounting firm's national managing partner for university relations and recruiting. "They also want systematic feedback from our more formal performance management and goal-setting systems." KPMG's Web-based Dialogue program includes a goal-setting form, project reviews, and interim and year-end evaluations that culminate with a final rating. For feedback on potential next steps in their careers, millennials can use KPMG's Employee Career Architecture, which includes an interactive mapping feature to explore future opportunities and the training and experiences required to qualify for them.

Millennials especially want mentors who will take a personal interest in them, help develop their skills, and show them how to navigate through the organization—and, yes of course, applaud them along the way for their achievements and career progress. In the KPMG survey of students, nearly a quarter said an active mentoring program would attract them to a company.

It's best to have multiple mentors. Official mentors may not have the time or desire to satisfy millennials' expectations for guidance. But millennials may be able to forge relationships with other colleagues who take a serious interest in their career growth. "This generation wants feedback throughout the year, and mentors can play a big part in that," says Carol Pledger, the head of Goldman Sachs University, the corporate training and development arm of Goldman Sachs Group Inc. New millennial hires at the investment banking firm are assigned both mentors and "buddies," colleagues who are slightly more senior, and they are encouraged to turn their own contacts into informal mentors as well.

"Mentors are not only a way of developing the millennials' skills, but they also make them feel connected to a company," says Mel Fugate, assistant professor in the Department of Management and Organizations at the Cox School of Business at Southern Methodist University. "Some formal mentoring programs are just there in name only, but when they're effective, they tell these young people that you do matter, you arc valuable to us." Without such feedback and mentoring, he adds, millennials "will become disengaged and less motivated and will eventually leave the company."

IBM has renewed its focus on mentoring in the last few years. New hires are first paired with a "connection coach" even before they begin working. Later they are matched with official mentors and encouraged to establish relationships with several more mentors, both inside and outside their geographical location and business unit. Millennials can choose mentors in three categories at IBM: expert, career guidance, and socialization. "Expert mentoring is really important with millennials because they want to expand their knowledge and increase their marketability within the company," Bing, IBM's director of learning, says. In addition, IBM offers "reverse mentoring" and "speed mentoring." Reverse mentoring pairs new millennial employees with executives who want to hear about the millennials' experiences and learn from them. At speed mentoring events, IBM employees spend a set amount of time with one person before moving on to the next. "People end up connecting not only with executives but also with their peers," Bing says. "They find people they never would have thought they'd want to connect with."

Catherine Solazzo, the young program manager at IBM, says mentors have played a part in all her promotions and awards. "They had seen promise in my performance over time and had line of sight to what my personal development goals were," says Solazzo, who checks in with her mentors regularly and works with them annually on her career goals. "They can candidly share their observations of your performance, which helps define your next steps and career moves," she says. "On a more personal level, my mentors also look out for my well-being. This gives you a feeling that they care about your happiness and development, as well as the company."

Other companies are increasing their career feedback, too, but they don't always call it mentoring. Deloitte & Touche says it wants to become a "coached organization." It believes that coaching resonates with millennials who don't want to be told what to do and are used to getting feedback from baseball coaches or vocal music coaches. At Deloitte, coaches are expected to listen closely and ask probing questions, but ultimately to lead employees to make career decisions themselves. "We view ourselves as a career enhancer, not necessarily a career destination," says Cathleen Benko, vice chairman and chief talent officer for Deloitte. "For the time that someone from the millennial generation is here with us, it's all about personal career growth and development."

Although large companies like Deloitte can afford to offer more elaborate mentoring or coaching resources, it may be harder to find a personal adviser at smaller businesses. But it isn't impossible. Paige Marino, who joined a consulting firm after receiving an M.B.A. degree from the University of California at Davis, worked on a few projects with a senior manager who ended up taking Marino under her wing and becoming an unofficial mentor. "She's the one I ask about company politics, which projects are good, and even my professional wardrobe and what it says about me," Marino says. "She seems genuinely concerned and does not hesitate to give me honest feedback and constructive criticism."

Mentoring isn't about getting her ego petted, Marino insists. "But someone needs to let you know right away if you're going down the wrong path. It is very important to me to do a good job and have people be pleased with my work."

CHAPTER HIGHLIGHTS

- The millennial generation craves feedback, especially praise, from their bosses on a regular basis. It keeps them engaged and motivated—and strongly increases the odds of retaining them.

- The generation's intense need for positive reinforcement in the workplace stems from their experiences as children and teenagers. Parents have praised millennials and made them feel special since birth, and both parent and child have been obsessed with achieving high grades in school.

- Millennials require careful handling when their performance isn't up to par. Harsh criticism can provoke tears—or even a resignation.

- More companies are providing formal performance reviews twice annually and encouraging managers to give millennials frequent informal progress reports throughout the year.

- Beyond performance reviews, millennials expect mentors, coaches, and training programs to help them develop their skills and rise to higher levels in the organization.

6

Checklist
Kids

The customer is all set to rent a car when he notices that his driver's license has expired. How should an auto rental agency employee handle such an unexpected complication? At Enterprise Rent-A-Car, where customer service is king, the response ought to be a no-brainer: offer to drive the customer to an office of the state department of motor vehicles to renew his license and then hand him the keys to his rental car.

But Enterprise is finding that young employees are often baffled by such snafus and must consult their supervisors about how to resolve them. "From day one on the job, we try to give our employees autonomy to think on their feet when dealing with customers," says Marie Artim, Enterprise's assistant vice president for recruiting. "But recent college graduates are struggling with autonomy and have more trouble making decisions than our management trainees did in the past. This generation wants someone's approval before proceeding with a decision."

In its training programs, Enterprise is encouraging its new recruits to think more independently, telling them that they should feel a sense of accomplishment when they take the initiative. "We tell them we understand that this is something new for them," Artim says, "but that they need to learn to run with it when confronted with a new situation."

The need for explicit direction is a common characteristic of the millennial generation. Many millennials struggle with independent thinking, decision making, and risk taking. They are especially flummoxed by unexpected, ambiguous challenges, the kind that business is all about. This tendency worries some educators and employers, who foresee a generation that can't cope well with the sudden twists and turns of their jobs and of life in general.

To be sure, millennials can be quite diligent once they have received clear directions. They bring to bear their technology savvy and can often work successfully on multiple projects at once. "But I think this generation will need additional help with critical decision-making skills and getting comfortable with ambiguity," says Stacey Rudnick, director of M.B.A. career services at the McCombs School of Business at the University of Texas in Austin. "M.B.A. programs may need to alter curricula over time to reflect the need for testing their independent decision-making skills."

In contrast to generation X, which "had a 'just do it' mentality and a bias toward action even without sufficient information, this generation seems to favor consensus and getting as much information as possible before making a decision," Rudnick adds. "They want to be right. That can be hard in business, where data are messy, decisions are complex, and there is almost never a perfect decision."

Of course, it is important to keep in mind that millennials aren't all the same. The desire for directions and checklists is certainly common among millennials, but it's not a universal trait. Two students I met at Seton Hall University illustrate well the different attitudes.

Joanna Ray is a more typical millennial. She simply loves checklists. "I have used checklists throughout my school years; in addition to having planners and homework assignment books, I would make my own list of things I had to accomplish for the day or week," says Ray, who was hired as a summer intern at Goldman Sachs Group Inc. and hopes eventually for a career in public relations and marketing, with a concentration in fashion. When she worked as a student assistant in Seton Hall's PR and marketing department, she received a list of assignments in the morning and checked them off as the day progressed. "Being able to cross off assignments," she says, "allows me to go home satisfied that I have had a productive day. I am a detail-oriented person and have more of a sense of accomplishment when I feel I have completed all that is expected of me."

Mark Saylor, in contrast, favors open-ended assignments and little direct supervision. "Wherever I end up working, I don't want a hovering boss," he says. "I work much better with time alone to figure things out. I don't have to be spoon fed." For a midterm project on the sociology of dating, for example, he says he rejected the standard term paper approach and wrote a humorous first-person piece of narrative fiction. His professor rewarded his creativity with a perfect grade.

Saylor, who majored in management and marketing, attributes his comfort with unstructured assignments to his childhood and his piano playing. An only child with working parents, he couldn't rely on them or siblings for entertainment and had to improvise instead. "I would play with toys and make up my own scenarios, which I believe fostered creativity," he says. As for the piano, he went beyond playing the notes on the sheet music to "emphasize different melodic lines and use dynamic, rhythmic changes to convey the message of the piece," he says. "I like to spread my wings and be creative."

PROGRAMMED LIVES

Saylor's upbringing is more the exception. Overly involved parents have caused many millennials to become highly dependent on directions and afraid of uncertainty and independent decision making. The so-called helicopter parents have been calling most of the shots from childhood through the college application process. They have programmed their kids' lives very carefully, filling every waking moment with play dates, music lessons, sports practices, tutors, and other structured activities. Millennials didn't have to be creative to fill their free time; there wasn't any. As for resolving problems and challenges in the classroom or on the playing field, parents typically intervened with teachers and coaches.

In school, millennials also have become accustomed to explicit directions. They have been taught very rigidly with detailed test guides and formulaic writing exercises so that they would score well on state achievement tests and college entrance exams. Teachers give them "rubrics" that spell out not only exactly what they're required to do for a project but also precisely how many points they will receive for each part that they get right—10 points for spelling and grammar, 25 points for written content, 15 points for the bibliography, and on and on. Teachers even include writing your name and the date as a project step so that students don't forget. What's more, teachers might award a couple of points for getting your own name and the date correct. Although these classroom rubrics give students precise checkpoints so that they understand exactly what's expected of them, such detailed guides can become a crutch that makes them overly dependent on specific instructions.

"Students were raised being told, 'Here's what's important and will be on the test,' rather than, 'We'll teach you the skills for how to think,'" says Marshall Pattie, director of student affairs at the Darden School of Business at the University of Virginia. He says students come into his office wanting to know how "everything will fit together, how all the different classes relate to one another, and how they will fit together in their life experience. They are really challenged by ambiguity and how to figure out how to fit things together."

Even after going away to college, millennials often experience little real autonomy and do little independent thinking because of being constantly connected by cell phone and text messaging to family and friends for advice and support. They also come to rely excessively on their professors and counselors for even the simplest decisions. Students pester professors with e-mail messages because they can't figure out how to tackle a writing assignment or can't decide something as elementary as which kind of notebook to buy for class.

"I get these looks of confusion and 'What do I do now?' if an assignment isn't completely straightforward," complains Jack Appleman, who teaches a media writing course at William Paterson University in Wayne, New Jersey. "They're unnerved when something is confusing and become impatient to fully understand everything right away. I think that sometimes ey're just too lazy to think." Most millennials aren't lazy; in fact, many have had much more homework during their school years than previous generations and have still made the high honor roll. But there's no denying that they often need and expect an undue amount of detailed guidance and support to get that homework done.

The need for direction isn't limited to class work. When some college students travel abroad, they treat professors like travel agents. That's how Faith Beasley, associate professor of French at Dartmouth College, feels sometimes. When a student arrived in Paris a day early, he sent her an e-mail asking for hotel recommendations. She politely suggested he consult the Internet or buy a tour book. He quickly e-mailed back and asked her to recommend specific online travel sites and books. She wrote back, "I'm not your travel agent. If you can't be more independent, I don't think you should be going to Paris." Offended, he shot back another message saying, "I thought you said you would be helpful."

So it goes these days for Beasley, who observes that it's a strain for even high achievers in the millennial generation to think independently and creatively. "They have a very hard time with literature courses where it's not mapped out and there are no right answers," she says. "They find it extremely frustrating that I can't give them an outline."

Admissions and career services offices also are dealing with many more checklist kids. Career services directors say millennial students find job searches taxing and often require extra support in making choices. Some schools are even hiring additional employees to provide more personalized career counseling to millennials. "Today's students very much want step-by-step checklists of how to find a job," says Jeffrey Rice, head of M.B.A. career services at the Fisher College of Business at Ohio State University. "So we give them a marketing plan and help them identify their strengths and the companies they are going to focus on in their search." When Rice takes students to Wall Street firms in New York City for interviews, he makes sure to give them a few basic rules on how to behave ("Stand up when the managing partner walks in the room" and "Use coasters for your drinks because you'll be sitting around a $50,000 conference table.")

The demand for direction can be a bit overwhelming. Jim Beirne, associate dean and director of the career center at the Olin Business School at Washington University in St. Louis, finds the requests for information very time consuming. "More than in the past, I am finding millennials asking for very straightforward, step-by-step directions, then after proceeding diligently through the steps, coming back shortly afterward, asking for the next level of step-by-step instructions," he says. "I sense a much deeper need for millennials to build parent-like relationship with our advisers."

Some college officials worry about students' lack of resourcefulness and wonder how they will cope in the workplace. Peter Johnson, M.B.A. admissions director at the Haas School of Business at the University of California at Berkeley, was amazed when a young man called to ask whether summer work counted as professional experience. "I would never call and ask an admissions director something like that," he says. "It shows lack of initiative because the information is readily available elsewhere. My concern is whether some of these young people are ready to solve business problems."

BOSSES OR BABYSITTERS?

Many millennials, in fact, aren't ready to grapple with complex business problems alone. Once they move into the workplace, they still want lots of hand holding. They flounder without precise guidelines but thrive in structured situations that provide clearly defined rules and the order that they crave. They like a straightforward road map and timeline of what their job responsibilities are and how they will pay off in terms of career advancement. That way, they figure, there will be no mistaking what they're expected to accomplish. In short, they want a clearly scripted work life. Of course, that's impossible in today's volatile business environment, but try telling that to a millennial.

So what's a manager to do with these checklist kids? At times, bosses may feel like overworked babysitters. After all, who has time to keep making lists and shepherding millennials so that they stay on task? But managers had better get used to it. They will have to spend many hours explaining their expectations as clearly as possible. Those expectations can be quite high; they just can't be vague. Managers will need to give step-by-step directions for handling everything from projects to voice-mail messages to client meetings. The bottom line is that you can't assume anything with millennials. It may seem obvious that employees should show up on time, limit lunchtime to an hour, and turn off cell phones during meetings. But those basics aren't necessarily apparent to many millennials. Their ignorance of workplace norms is sometimes truly astounding.

Used to relying on parents and teachers to keep them on track to meet deadlines, some millennials now expect the same close oversight from managers. They need someone to tell them what to do next and to keep reminding them when it's due. Gail McDaniel, a corporate consultant and career coach for college students, spoke to managers at a health care company who were frustrated by some of their millennial employees. It seems that one young man missed an important deadline, and when his manager asked him to explain, he said, "Oh, you forgot to remind me."

Parents and teachers aren't doing millennials any favors by constantly adapting to their needs, McDaniel says. "Going into the workplace, they have an expectation that companies will adapt for them, too. These kids become accustomed to specific tasks being laid out for them and don't want to take personal responsibility." Her solution: managers must put more emphasis on explaining in detail how a millennial's work affects the big picture at the company and what the consequences will be if a deadline is missed.

Some management experts advise companies to start out by giving their new millennial hires short-term deadlines. As they improve their time management skills, perhaps through corporate training programs, they should be able to handle longer-range projects without so much direction and supervision. Some managers also find it useful to tell millennials to at least brainstorm some possible solutions before running to them for advice about every little complication.

A SCARED GENERATION

Business schools and companies find that millennials are indecisive and need direction partly because they're afraid to take risks and make mistakes. They have been sheltered from failure by their parents and are nervous about making a bold decision that could end up being a blunder and a disappointment to their families, teachers, and bosses. "Creativity scares me," a member of the millennial generation told me. "I think we are a scared generation, scared to take risks, scared to think independently for fear it may produce ridiculous ideas. We are a generation that seeks approval."

When a recruiter asked M.B.A. students to describe the biggest risks they have taken, most said that it was quitting their jobs to go to business school. She laughed because their responses showed how little risk they have been exposed to in their 20-plus years.

Lisa Feldman, recruiting director at Berkeley's Haas School of Business, also senses risk aversion when she counsels students. She has taken to putting career information and even e-mails in checklist form because students follow them to the letter and find them reassuring. "Millennials want to do it right and are very obedient when we give them checklists," she says. But they still need her guidance for unexpected developments that aren't on any of her checklists. They may figure out the best approach to a problem but still want her to give them the final approval and the push that they need to take action.

"I received an e-mail from a student who had to cancel an interview and was afraid of doing it wrong," Feldman says. "I think, 'Oh my goodness, can they not figure it out themselves?'" What really annoyed her was the student who called her at home one evening, panicked because he didn't know how to resolve his dilemma of two conflicting job interviews. To get her cell phone number, he had called Feldman's office and said it was an emergency—even though the interviews were five days away. "I told him, 'You have to make a decision, and don't call me at home again,'" she says.

TOO MUCH TEAMWORK

Millennials work well together—maybe too well. Companies will find that millennials are team players extraordinaire. They have spent much of their lives working in groups at school and in extracurricular activities, all of which makes them a good fit for universities and companies that value teamwork.

But teamwork partly accounts for their weakness in taking risks and thinking creatively and independently. They like the collegiality of teamwork and feel comfortable relying on the entire team to provide direction and keep everyone on track. They also prefer to reach a group consensus rather than make difficult decisions on their own. Team decisions are safer, less risky to the individual.

But where are the leaders? With their groupthink mentality, millennials may not make outstanding leaders. The team player mindset and team style of working are fine for many business projects, but companies also are looking for other traits in their future leaders. They want employees who are poised to take risks and think creatively on their own to solve thorny problems. More than ever, business managers and executives must be adaptable and prepared to manage change in today's fast-moving global economy. With millennials so averse to ambiguity and risk, many companies worry whether this generation will be up to the challenge.

According to a 2007 survey of corporate recruiters by *The Wall Street Journal* and Harris Interactive, many millennials may be lacking just what recruiters are looking for most these days: 9 out of 10 recruiters said they are increasingly seeking students who are versatile and adaptable to change. "Too many people think life and work come with a rule book," one recruiter commented.

Some companies believe colleges and M.B.A. programs have gone overboard in emphasizing teamwork. They would like to see more encouragement of independent decision making. A financial services industry recruiter cringes when she reads yet another cover letter about how great a team player the applicant is. "I say, 'Shoot! What we need are independent thinkers and creative people who aren't always trying to get consensus,'" she says. "I want people who will take the initiative and take some risks."

Owen Hannay, who heads up the Slingshot advertising agency in Dallas, finds that his millennial generation employees have trouble taking personal responsibility for a project. They shy away from accepting responsibility because they have been so used to working in teams and consulting family or friends on even minor decisions in their lives. "Many times," he says, "we have given an assignment to a writer–art director team and found a large group downstairs working together on the project. It can often result in better work, but it takes time away from what the rest of the group have been assigned and completely blows the cost structure of the project."

If millennials are forced to be personally accountable for a project and it doesn't turn out well, the disappointing experience can rock their lives. "What is unique about them," Hannay says, "is that they come out of college in many cases without ever having failed, or if they have, they have not taken any personal responsibility for that failure."

To help his young employees adjust to the realities of the workplace, Hannay turned to his alma mater, the Cox School of Business at Southern Methodist University. The school created a customized executive education program for Slingshot that covered a number of issues, including time management and project management. "Companies like Slingshot look at custom programs as organizational interventions," says Frank Lloyd, associate dean of executive education at the Cox School. "They have a lot of new young people and need to get them all on the same page."

GETTING COMFORTABLE WITH THE GRAY

Like Slinghot, many companies are spending more time trying to wean millennials from their need for detailed directions and teach them to deal better with the gray areas of life. At Boston Consulting Group Inc., the management consultants must possess an aptitude for dealing with ambiguity and creating order from scattered information. But the firm finds that some millennials require more than the usual training and structure to learn to handle ambiguity. In training programs conducted before they're sitting across from a client, young consultants must grapple with simulated management problems to become more comfortable working without a paint-by-numbers manual. They learn to develop hypotheses and break chaotic problems into more manageable units.

"Much of our work is bringing order to chaos," says Ian Frost, Boston Consulting's partner for training and development in the Americas. "But some people are almost paralyzed if they don't know what to do next. We help train them to define the problem and come up with a hypothesis and work plan to solve it. Over time, they get better and better at it."

Like other management consulting firms, Boston Consulting has long put applicants through "case-study interviews" to discover who is most adept at handling ambiguity.

Applicants are given some facts about a real-world management problem and must develop a recommendation for a fictitious client. "It's a very discerning tool," says Kermit King, senior partner and head of recruiting for the Americas. "We can have two students, both with embarrassingly excellent resumes. One will get lost in the case; the other will conquer the ambiguity. It's puzzling."

King finds that millennials can be excellent at synthesizing information and coming up with relevant solutions. "But their managers must say clearly what needs to be accomplished," he says, "and check in frequently to provide them with structure." Too much direction, though, can be damaging. "We have to be careful," he adds, "not to impose so much structure that it stifles their ingenuity."

King believes that the millennial generation gets a bad rap for its need for guidance. "I believe our undergraduates get smarter every year," he says. "They may need more direction, but it's a caricature to depict them as unable to take a step forward without looking at their feet and getting help from their helicopter parents."

Other employers aren't quite as sanguine about the millennials. The financial services industry worries about the millennials' discomfort with taking risks in uncertain situations. Recruiters for Fidelity Investments, for example, are quite concerned to find that so many students today are reluctant to take risks and make independent decisions. Fidelity managers believe that millennials have so often sought advice and consensus that they have graduated from college with virtually no experience in making major decisions on their own.

Risk taking, creativity, flexibility, and independent thinking are critical attributes for Fidelity, of course, because its business is all about making informed judgments and taking risks in selecting stocks to invest in. Before hiring millennial generation students, Fidelity recruiters try to screen for an ability to deal well with ambiguity and to think creatively and independently. For example, it asks summer intern candidates to evaluate a stack of material on a retailing company in order to see how quickly they can sift through the information, determine which facts are relevant, and then decide whether to buy or sell the company's stock.

Fidelity believes that in time it can mold millennials to be more comfortable with risk and ambiguity. Through in-house training programs and on-the-job experiences, the company tries to encourage graduates to be more willing to take the initiative, even if they sometimes make errors. Managers tell young recruits that mistakes are expected and to be learned from. They also point out that employees fail more because they can't make a decision than because of mistakes.

Some millennials also believe that they can overcome their fear of risk and uncertainty. Although they acknowledge their anxiety when faced with open-ended, ambiguous work projects, they feel that it may simply take them longer at first to find their way without a map. David Iannone, a graduate of the University of Connecticut, felt a bit lost and scared at first when he started working at a marketing agency. His new tobacco account didn't come with a "job description or any clear delineation of my responsibilities," he says, leaving him unsure about exactly how to proceed. He tried to be patient, use intuition, and ask a lot of questions to clarify his assignment.

Iannone knows he faces many more uncharted assignments and is working on his time management and organizational skills. "Don't get me wrong," he concedes. "I am definitely a procrastinator. But over the years, I've managed to bend and maximize the time that I choose to use; I look at time as 24 hours rather than a normal clock" of 9-to-5 work hours.

Although Iannone says he's a very disorganized person who can't keep track of "my bills, my papers, or my life," he can always locate vital information at the office. "Some call it packratting; I call it archiving," he says. "Regardless, it helps me simplify complex, unrelated problems by always having documentation of something that's needed."

To manage the never ceasing daily flood of information, Iannone first writes everything down in a five-subject notebook. The first section contains his daily to-do lists and "everything important." He dates every page of his notes and labels them with a subject heading. Then he types up a recap on his computer with "the high-level aspects of what was covered and any actionable next steps that need to be taken." It's hard for him to stay on top of this task, but it forces him to boil information down to the core ideas.

"It was a painful search to figure all that out, but I feel more comfortable now about what I should be doing," Iannone says. "I would have to say that working in a less structured environment is exciting. I like the challenge of making something from nothing and distilling chaos into order. But the process can also be stressful and full of anxiety."

AMBIGUITY 101

Business schools may be able to reduce the stress and anxiety. By adjusting their curriculum and teaching methods, they can help students become more adept at dealing with ambiguous situations. For one thing, they can tone down their emphasis on teamwork and collaborative decision making. They can also assign students more open-ended projects with fewer instructions and less clear-cut outcomes.

Traditional business case studies could provide students with a rich opportunity for creative thinking to resolve prickly management problems. But often the cases come complete with all the relevant information and don't leave much room for independent judgment. Because most case studies are just too tidy, Columbia University's business school has created "decision briefs" that offer less information and leave more room for exploration and innovative thinking. The goal is to simulate the real workplace and spur decision making based on less than perfect data. For example, M.B.A. students watched a video interview with a General Electric Co. executive about problems facing its business-process outsourcing division in India. Then they formulated possible strategies in class before viewing a second video describing GE's solution.

Other schools are offering new courses in problem-solving strategies. For its recently revised first-year curriculum, the Yale School of Management added an "individual problem framing" course. It includes lessons on simplifying problems, breaking problems down into parts, and searching for related problems that an individual already knows how to solve. "We want to get students to understand how to structure an unstructured situation," says Joel Podolny, dean of Yale's management school.

Some schools give students practical projects to expose them to ambiguity. The Ross School of Business at the University of

Michigan requires that all its M.B.A. students complete a seven-week "multidisciplinary action project" to gain practical, real-world problem-solving experience. The assignments range from helping Lord & Taylor department stores develop a strategy for increasing market penetration to determining whether Rwanda can produce infant formula as an alternative to breast milk for HIV-positive mothers.

Whatever the project, the goal is the same: to think analytically and creatively in situations where you might have less information than you'd like and where the variables may change. But not everyone likes the open-ended, unpredictable nature of the projects. "We teach not just problem solving but also opportunity, innovation, and creativity by giving students projects that aren't clearly defined," says Robert Dolan, dean of the Ross School. "Some students get frustrated and say their project isn't well defined, and we say, 'Yeah, that's sort of the point.'"

Charmaine Courtis, executive director of student services and international relations at the Schulich School of Business at York University in Toronto, finds much the same reaction to the strategic consulting projects that students there must undertake for real clients. Many students struggle with the projects, which demand creative problem-solving skills and entrepreneurial thinking. "Younger people today have real trouble with ambiguity," she says. "But the strategic study is extremely important because it shows them that things are rarely black and white in business or in life."

CHAPTER HIGHLIGHTS

- The millennial generation thrives on structure and explicit directions. Give these young people a checklist, and they're sure to get the job done.

- Because they received so much support from parents and teachers through the years, many millennials struggle to think independently and deal with ambiguous situations.

- Managers need to provide millennials with an unusual amount of hand holding, reminding them of project deadlines and telling them such elementary things as the importance of turning off cell phones during client meetings.

- Millennials are risk averse and fearful of making mistakes, having relied so much on team consensus in classrooms and on the job. They require encouragement to take some chances and learn from their inevitable mistakes.

- Some companies are trying to help millennials become more comfortable with ambiguity by teaching them how to break problems into more manageable units and how to determine which data are most relevant to the solution.

- Recognizing the millennial generation's need for direction and clarity, business schools are challenging students to tackle more open-ended problems in both the classroom and in real-world field projects.

7

Master
Jugglers

Jaclyn DeCicco considers herself a member of generation M—that's "M" for multitasking, not millennial. Oh, she's a millennial, too. But she particularly takes pride in declaring herself a "master multitasker." She travels frequently for her job in the university recruiting and relations department at International Business Machines Corp., and she swears she'd never survive if she weren't adept at balancing four or five activities at once.

Here's how she might spend her time at an airport in between business trips: she would be listening in on a teleconference call with her colleagues and manager, catching up on e-mail, responding to half a dozen instant messages, chatting with another IBM employee seated next to her, and squeezing in a quick business call on her cell phone. Whew!

But it's no sweat for this millennial multitasker, who considers such juggling all in a day's work. "There is so much to be done during any given day that if I couldn't maximize multitasking, I'd be working around the clock," says DeCicco, who is in her mid-20s. "Frankly, it's hard to imagine not being able to do a million things at once."

DeCicco and her fellow millennials are indeed the ultimate plugged-in multitaskers. Perhaps the most distinctive attributes of the millennial generation are their technology savvy and their agility in handling multiple pursuits at once. Millennials not only stay connected 24/7 through technology, but like DeCicco, they also want to be engaged simultaneously in a myriad of experiences.

They can't stand doing homework all alone in a quiet room. While they're studying, they also need to be text messaging a friend, listening to their favorite tunes on an iPod, checking out the latest developments on another friend's Facebook page, and heating up a bag of popcorn in the microwave.

In a study conducted by the Kaiser Family Foundation, nearly a third of 8- to 18-year-olds said they talk on the phone, send instant messages, watch television shows, listen to music, or surf the Web for fun "most of the time" while they're finishing their homework. Through such multitasking, the young people said they manage to pack more total media time into their day. Roughly a quarter of them said they use other media most of the time while watching television or reading, and a third said they are usually "media multitasking" when listening to music or logging on to a computer.

There is debate over the pros and cons of multitasking. On one hand, it allows millennials to have more experiences, make more connections, and perhaps even enhance productivity, at least for some tasks. On the other hand, spending too much time multitasking and connecting online can be distracting and can detract from learning and communicating effectively in writing and in personal interactions.

Most millennials, though, see only the upside of technology and multitasking. Understandably, technology is the lifeblood of the millennials, who came of age along with the Internet and cellular phones. For much of their lives, they have been connected to the world through online video games, mobile phones, e-mail, text messages, BlackBerries, iPods, and other digital wonders. They have become enthralled with social networking sites like MySpace and have created fantasy lives for themselves in Second Life and other virtual online worlds. They love listening to podcasts and reading blogs, and they are communicating in ever shorter conversational bites on "microblogs." Indeed, it takes multitasking skills just to keep up with the newest of the new technologies and social media. In describing millennials' affinity for technology, one corporate recruiter told me, "They were born with a computer in their hands and learned to use Google before the dictionary."

To attract millennials, companies will need to satisfy this addiction to technology and multitasking. "Young people today expect to apply the same social networking skills at work that they've been using in school and their personal lives," says Eric Lesser, associate partner for global business services at IBM. "Millennials who have been instant messaging since middle school want to walk into the workplace and start connecting immediately. But if a company says we don't want you wasting time on instant messaging and social networks, there will be an instant disconnect."

Just how connected are millennials? The Pew Research Center in Washington, DC, surveyed 18- to 25-year-olds and found that more than half had used a social networking site and 44% had created a personal profile. More than two-thirds said they believe new technologies make it easier to find new friends. In addition to connecting with friends, millennials rely on social networking sites for political information. In a separate Pew study, 37% of 18- to 24-year-olds said they gleaned campaign information from such sites as MySpace and Facebook.

Millennials aren't just passive voyeurs on the Internet. They also have become prolific content creators. According to Pew, nearly two-thirds of online teens have created content on the Internet. Girls are busier than boys with blogging (35% versus 20%), but boys post more videos online (19% versus 10%).

Millennials, of course, are big consumers of technology gizmos. What is especially fascinating is how millennials have emotionally bonded with these gadgets, especially their cell phones. They say they would feel utterly helpless and cut off from the world without their mobile phones. For a research study, the JWT advertising agency asked some millennials to write about their phones and learned just how passionately they feel. A young woman named Alice wrote, "This sounds crazy, but it's true: My first love was my first cell phone. I called her Mercedes. . . . My favorite thing about Mercedes was her sweet, simple ring. I loved the fact that she provided me with a link to the outside world while I sat within the walls of my boring suburban high school." Another young woman named Bailey described her first cell phone as "a symbol of independence, freedom. Like the 'keys to the house' for the 21st century. Almost as good as getting one's driver's license. For some reason, this little gadget . . . gave me the feeling that

I could now go anywhere and always be able to get out of trouble."

Millennials are so tied to technology tools that they may be 10 feet away from you but still send a text message or e-mail rather than simply call out to you. Millennials have even been known to quit their jobs by e-mail. Yet as many impatient millennials might say, e-mail is sooo dead. It's the new snail mail. Millennials expect rapid-fire feedback and get bored in a New York minute. No, make that a nanosecond.

Now, texting on cell phones, instant messaging, and sending messages on social networking sites have become their preferred modes of communication. According to the Pew Research Center, about half of 18- to 25-year-old survey respondents said they had sent or received a text message on a cell phone in the previous 24-hour period, compared with only 10% of baby boomers. In Japan, young women are even composing "cell phone novels" on their keypads, writing the best-selling love stories in short text-message-style sentences.

Older generations are trying to keep pace with millennials, but many colleges and companies aren't yet up to speed. Some colleges have begun offering a limited amount of instant messaging in their admissions and career services offices, though it's far from widespread. In the corporate world, some managers see the productivity benefits from faster electronic communication, but millennials will be disappointed to find that e-mail still rules in many workplaces.

IBM's Jaclyn DeCicco couldn't even imagine working for a company stuck in the prehistoric e-mail era. Logging on to IBM's instant messaging system is the very first thing the university relations specialist does each morning when she arrives at her office. She has been instant messaging since her first day of college and finds it critical to her efficiency and productivity. "Without it," she says, "I'd spend much more time writing tedious e-mails and on very long teleconferences."

As for multitasking, DeCicco considers it her generation's special talent. "Since older generations are still learning to use the new tools, the likelihood of them being able to juggle an instant messaging meeting, e-mail, and a mobile call simultaneously is pretty slim," she says. "It can take someone from an older generation much longer to catch on to new technology, so it's important for me to have patience and be able to teach tips and tricks that make their learning curve smaller."

INTERACTIVE INSTRUCTION

Multitasking millennials expect the latest technologies wherever they go, and that includes the classroom. They may have to turn off their cell phones, iPods, and game players when they reach the classroom door, but they certainly don't expect the multimedia experience to stop there.

Indeed, millennials are the driving force behind a push in education to provide both technology and entertainment that will hold students' attention long enough to get through a 45-minute lesson. Some teachers and corporate recruiters worry that all the multimedia bells and whistles are diluting the academic content and weakening students' basic reading, writing, and math skills. Nevertheless, schools are plunging ahead with more interactive and multisensory teaching techniques.

To keep students actively focused on the lesson, some K–12 school districts are playing to their love of games and their text messaging skills. Forget paper-and-pencil quizzes. Now, teachers are handing out clickers to students, who punch in their answers to questions and see a tally of the entire class's responses on a big screen in the front of the room. Besides their appealing interactive technology, the remote-control gadgets let teachers monitor everyone's performance, including quiet students who don't normally raise their hands.

The Internet is making it easier for teachers to find tools to motivate this video generation. YouTube-like Web sites, for example, provide them with short, ready-made videos to play in class. Videos on the TeacherTube site might include "Eggsplosion," a lively chemistry experiment involving filling an egg with hydrogen gas and lighting it; images of spheres, cubes, cones, and other shapes flashing on the screen to the beat of dance-club music; and a history teacher's version of the game show *Jeopardy*. Schools sometimes even assign online instructional videos as homework to help reinforce a math or science concept.

At the university level, schools are embracing technology in a variety of ways because they know that college students will simply walk out on a dry lecture and never return. Wireless Internet access is now common across many campuses, allowing students to log on almost anywhere. Schools are putting more lectures in audio and video formats that students can download to their computers or iPods, and professors often post class notes and other information online for students to access at their convenience. The downside of such handy online lessons: more empty seats during the live class.

For the students who do show up for class, the amount of innovation and technology may surprise them. Hoping to capture the fleeting attention of the easily distracted millennials, colleges are adopting more entertaining and interactive approaches, such as videos, podcasts, audio clips, blogs, computer games, and talk-show formats that encourage more discussion than a straight lecture. There also are classroom role-playing simulations that are more interactive than a printed lesson.

"How do you hold students for a two-hour class when they have two-minute attention spans?" asks Lenie Holbrook, an associate professor of management systems at Ohio University, who incorporates movies and music into some of his classes. "We have no choice but to change our approach as our audience changes." To spark discussion of everything from control to career planning to work-life balance, he plays recordings of songs by Janet Jackson, Pink Floyd, John Mayer, and the Police. He also shows clips from movies, such as the animated *Madagascar*, which he uses to examine the liabilities of group decision making.

Universities are concerned about reaching millennials outside the classroom, too. Some professors have moved to "virtual office hours," chatting with students online by text, microphone, or Webcam. To try to provide reliable sexual information to millennial students, Indiana University's Kinsey Institute has expanded beyond its weekly column in college newspapers and created the Kinsey Confidential blog, three-minute podcasts, and a Kinsey Facebook group.

Some business schools are linking up with technology companies to create a multimedia learning experience. So-called serious games are being tested at Brandeis University's business school in Waltham, Massachusetts, in partnership with IBM. The three-dimensional video game Innov8, for example, was designed to teach students a combination of business and information technology skills. In France, the HEC School of Management joined with Apple Inc. to give all M.B.A. students a video iPod for access to lectures, notes, tutorials, library resources, and other information. Students can also view recordings of their own class presentations on the iPod and work with professors and coaches to polish their communication skills.

Second Life, the three-dimensional virtual world with more than 13 million "residents," called avatars, has begun attracting the attention of more colleges and business schools. For business schools, Second Life provides the opportunity to study a virtual economy with its own marketplace and money. That appealed to Insead, which has actual business school campuses in France and Singapore. The school has established a virtual Second Life campus with plans to offer an M.B.A. class on entrepreneurship in which students can develop and test business plans in the online community. "We recognize the growing importance of the digital marketplace and want all of our participants to have the opportunity to experience it first-hand," says Antonio Fatas, dean of Insead's M.B.A. program.

Case studies remain a primary teaching tool in business schools, but Yale University's M.B.A. program is creating more cases with multimedia content rather than printed materials. For example, a study of the high-stakes takeover battle for Equity Office Properties Trust includes an online trove of newspaper articles, news videos, financial documents, stock charts, video interviews with the principals in the case, securities analysts' reports, even Google maps and photographs of Equity's office buildings. "This generation thinks in hyperlinks," says Joel Podolny, dean of the Yale School of Management. "If I give a student a 20-page case study, he complains that it's too long. Yet he has no problem with more than 1,000 pages worth of content that he can navigate through online."

But this plugged-in generation's technology can be a mixed blessing for professors. To enrich the classroom learning experience, students can delve deeply into the financial performance of a company by opening spreadsheets on their laptops and mining for data on the Internet. But they also can surreptitiously send an instant message, play online games, or check out a classmate's Facebook page, missing out entirely on the professor's lecture and class discussion. There also are concerns that students can use laptops, cell phones, and even social networking groups to cheat more easily. Some professors are circulating around their rooms more often to observe students' behavior up close and are even cutting off Internet access during their classes to keep students from getting distracted or cheating.

MOVING AT THEIR OWN SPEED

In many ways, the multitasking millennial generation is extremely well prepared to move from college into the 21st-century workplace. At first, companies may find their need for a constant swirl of activity and for multisensory, rapid-fire communication jarring. But millennials will help satisfy the workplace's growing demand for technological prowess.

They will clearly be of great value to their employers with their knowledge of computer software applications, their global connections via the Internet, and their desire to work on multiple projects at once. Corporate recruiters say that these new hires should be so well versed, for example, in software tools for financial analysis and business modeling that they will be able to concentrate on other skills, such as learning to manage client relationships.

Ambitious millennials want their careers to move at an accelerated pace, and believe that technology gives them an edge. For them, it's only natural to use several technologies simultaneously to get the job done better and faster. Consider, for example, Mark Kull, the young financial representative for Northwestern Mutual Life Insurance Co. in Louisville, Kentucky, who exploits technology to cultivate new clients and then develop personal relationships with them.

He has recruited clients in distant states, using e-mail and online meeting technology. To forge a closer bond with them, he might send text messages during a baseball game, commenting on a great play and sending his best wishes. For Kull, social networking is more than social. He views his Facebook friends as future business opportunities. "Social networking is unbelievable for my business," he says. "If a friend gets a job at Exxon Mobil, he goes from being just a good friend to being a heck of a great prospect."

Millennials believe they are sometimes unfairly pegged as lazy when they are simply pros at multitasking and using technology to find shortcuts. "I can get some tasks done in 10 minutes instead of an hour because of technology," Kull says. "But that is not about having less work ethic."

Multitasking and technology contribute to the millennials' reputation for impatience in the workplace. Indeed, Mike Lach, a millennial and a material engineer in Los Angeles, is proud of his impatient streak. He gets bored easily with a single project and needs multiple assignments to stay engaged.

"We are able to multitask so effectively that we tend to skim over the communication details with older generations whose pace is much slower," he says. "My boss will spend half an hour on a three-sentence e-mail to get it just right, but I communicate fine in a looser way." Lach also grows weary of running time-consuming spreadsheets when he believes that the solution is obvious. "We find that sort of thing very tedious and a way that older generations show their authority," he says. "I like a more entrepreneurial spirit in a company. I feel like I should be able to multitask as fast as I'm able and go home when the work is finished, even if that's in the middle of the afternoon."

CORPORATE CONNECTIONS

By the time they reach the workplace, millennials like Kull and Lach expect companies to give them on-the-job access to the same technologies they used in college and have long enjoyed in their personal lives. That, of course, presents a big challenge for many companies, but gives some employers, particularly in the technology field, a distinct advantage in recruiting this generation. Such companies as Google Inc., Microsoft Corp., Apple, and IBM can meet this generation's high-tech networking needs much better than many other industries.

At IBM, for example, millennials like Jaclyn DeCicco, the young university relations specialist, revel in all the technology and social networking connections at their fingertips. The social networking world at IBM includes more than 10,000 blogs and 15,000 wikis, which are knowledge-sharing Web sites that people can freely edit or add content to. Thousands of employees also share lists of their favorite Web sites and corporate resources with an IBM program for "social bookmarking" called DogEar. The company boasts a major presence in the Second Life virtual community and uses its "islands" there for lectures, group discussions, and other activities. There also are online brainstorming sessions called "jams." IBM's Innovation Jam in 2006 attracted 140,000 employees, family members, clients, and business partners, and yielded ideas for 10 new projects.

DeCicco uses wikis to keep her colleagues and other teams in the loop about what's happening at the dozens of campuses where IBM recruits. She especially likes the company's internal social networking site called Beehive, where employees share photos and messages with each other. She also uses Facebook for both work and personal matters and connects through Google Groups with fellow students in a part-time master's degree program at New York University. "It's neat to see a blend of colleagues and friends in the same space," she says.

IBM considers its workplace technologies and social networking culture vital selling points with the millennial generation. "They're entering the workforce so comfortable with technology and so adaptable to any piece of software we put in front of them," says John Rooney, manager of technology adoption at IBM. "They like our open culture, which allows them to determine the rules of conversation and who they will reach out to. We'll see posts at our BlogCentral to our senior executives from people relatively new to IBM, questioning a business strategy or expressing disappointment about something in their work environment."

Other companies may not be able to match IBM's workplace offerings, but they are starting to develop more technology and networking tools, from instant messaging to wikis to internal social networking sites. Capital One Financial Corp. is trying to increase networking and collaboration by creating internal discussion boards and its own version of Wikipedia, the online encyclopedia. The goal is to encourage workers to break out of their job function silos and network virtually with colleagues throughout Capital One in solving problems and completing projects. The new networking tools will be self-monitored, meaning that employees can flag and remove inappropriate content, as well as correct false information in the encyclopedia of Capital One reference terms.

"The students we hire are used to having wi-fi networks and walking around campus with their backpacks, laptops, and cell phones," says Matthew Schuyler, the chief human resources officer at Capital One. "You will struggle to recruit millennials if you don't replicate that mobile, multitasking environment in the workplace with technology and social networking tools. They'll say, 'Are you kidding?' if you show them a landline phone to use. It's a very foreign concept to millennials."

Sometimes the millennials themselves are the impetus for innovation. Young M.B.A. graduates at Johnson & Johnson, for instance, successfully lobbied to get their own social networking site so that they could stay in touch with each other. Connecting isn't always easy in a global, decentralized company like Johnson & Johnson, so an online community seemed only natural. Now, millennial M.B.A.s can contribute to a blog on the i-Link site, and the company has begun using it as a virtual classroom for training and a career center for counseling. "The idea came out of a focus group with millennials for our senior managers," says Kaye Foster-Cheek, vice president for human resources. "But those millennials weren't going to sit back and wait for me to find a solution for connecting; they went on and built it for themselves."

Johnson & Johnson expects eventually to broaden its social networking beyond M.B.A.s. Already, a few companies have launched corporation-wide sites that they hope will connect millennials not only with each other but with older generations as well. Deloitte & Touche calls its internal networking program D Street and promotes it as "one degree of separation" from other employees of the firm. The accounting firm's employees can blog, share photographs, search colleagues' profiles, and connect with people of interest. "D Street is like a storefront for people to show who they are to the rest of Deloitte," says Cathleen Benko, vice chairman and chief talent officer. "If you're looking for someone familiar with the cosmetics industry who also speaks French, you can go to D Street and bingo, find a match in our organization."

Corporate training also is going digital. To train the young sales staffs at sporting goods stores, Nike Inc. developed "Sports Knowledge Underground," an interactive Web-based program that is modeled on a subway system. Different train routes lead to various lessons on selling and to information about Nike shoes and equipment.

To make corporate learning more portable, some companies are developing training podcasts that employees can download to cell phones, laptops, BlackBerries, and iPods. Investment bankers at Merrill Lynch & Co., for instance, can use their BlackBerries to take a series of training courses on such topics as information risk and preventing money laundering. In a pilot test of the program, bankers completed Merrill's GoLearn BlackBerry training in 45% less time on average and scored slightly higher on final assessment tests than other employees at the firm. The bankers liked being able to do their training while traveling, as well as at other times when they didn't have any work distractions.

Companies increasingly realize that millennials won't tolerate being digitally disconnected even for a moment. During an orientation program for business school recruits in Bangalore, India, Wipro Technologies had to scramble to keep them connected to their families and friends. Many of the most popular networking sites were blocked for security reasons, causing some consternation among the millennials. Wipro managed to open a few sites and also provided the millennials with individual phones they could use to make calls over the Internet. "The experience really reinforced for us the fact that millennials are the most connected generation in history and always want to stay connected," says Vishu Venkat, manager of strategic resourcing for the Indian information technology services company.

Still, some employers are playing Big Brother and blocking Web technologies from the workplace, whether it ruffles the millennials' feathers or not. Web sites with sexual content have long been off-limits at many companies. Now, some companies are cracking down on all video watching, including YouTube, to prevent employees from wasting time. They also fear that their computer networks might crash because they have limited bandwidth capacity to accommodate video files.

Despite the benefits of real-time communication and the potential for greater collaboration, some technophobic companies still refuse to provide instant messaging capabilities. Instant messaging bans, which are sometimes a result of legal and security concerns, are sure to annoy millennials. They also won't be drawn to companies that block social networking sites. Nearly two-thirds of employers deny access to MySpace, Facebook, and similar sites, according to a 2007 survey by Clearswift, a content security firm.

That may be shortsighted thinking. Employers should reconsider policies barring workers from networking at popular sites like Facebook or LinkedIn. Not only could such bans drive millennials away, but the companies also could miss business opportunities. The millennials' social connections just might turn into valuable new customers or recruits someday.

NO PRIVACY

Log on to a personal profile on Facebook or MySpace and don't be surprised to see a topless young woman in a suggestive pose or a barely clad young man chugging a beer. The exhibitionists will probably also be sharing steamy details of their latest sexual conquests. What if those were your employees? Maybe they are.

Millennials are an open book, incredibly uninhibited and oblivious to boundaries. They show little sense of discretion in their willingness to tell all and show all, whether in blogs, on gossip sites like Juicy Campus, or on their own social networking pages. Their online connections and conversations are making waves in the workplace, causing employers to shake their heads over this generation's lack of propriety and privacy. Millennials simply don't have the same filters for censoring personal information that older generations do.

Although millennials' transparency can be refreshing at times, they're often far too free with information online about what they did on last night's date or what a corporate recruiter asked them in an interview. For employers, this lack of privacy creates a temptation to snoop and get a more intimate view of job applicants than their resumes provide. Some companies insist that they have policies against prying into people's online lives, but others think that it's fair game to investigate job prospects to avoid hiring a bad apple.

"The online world works both ways," says Benko, the chief talent officer for Deloitte. "We are finding new ways of communicating with potential recruits online, but we also feel that we can tap Facebook and other sites to learn more about potential employees. It provides a window into who they are and gives us a lot more information in making hiring decisions."

It's hard to remove content once it's floating out there in cyberspace, but it's critical that millennials at least delete any inappropriate language or indecent pictures from all their current online profiles. They also should ensure that their e-mail addresses and other electronic user names are tasteful. "We are talking to students and instructing them in more detail about their online identity," says Stacey Rudnick, director of M.B.A. career services at the McCombs School of Business at the University of Texas in Austin. "Do they know what is out there on them via MySpace, Facebook, YouTube, and Google? Images, video, and personal blogs are all fair game for an inquisitive alumnus or recruiter."

The lack of privacy doesn't just hurt millennials. Companies can be burned, too, by millennials' need for self-expression and their naive openness online. Millennials may believe they can use business laptops, cell phones, and BlackBerries for personal communication, including online gossip. Employers must therefore remind them that if they're text messaging or chatting on company equipment, they should keep it clean and stick to business matters.

Some millennials also recklessly post negative comments about companies on recruiting Web sites, such as Vault.com. That could ruin their reputations not only with the company they're assailing but also with other recruiters who don't approve of such public venting.

Rudnick recalls a student who posted all the questions from her interviews with a company on a recruiting Web site in response to another student's online query. She also foolishly included details about her negative experiences during the interviews. Unbeknownst to her, she was actually about to get an offer from the firm. Then the company happened to see her posting, which included her personal, easily recognizable e-mail address. In the end, the job offer never materialized.

THE INTERNET GENERATION'S DISCONNECTIONS

Although the millennial generation's attitude seems to be the more stimulation the better, too much multitasking may actually prove harmful. It could be undermining critical concentration, reading, communication, and interpersonal skills. Some critics even consider the millennials' extreme multitasking a manifestation of attention deficit disorder and have labeled them the Ritalin Generation.

There's no question that some multitaskers have short attention spans and are easily distracted and bored. Although adroit multitasking might mean greater productivity on routine projects, it might not result in top-flight work for assignments that require focus, critical analysis, and deeper thinking. Employers should be alert to excessive multitasking and rein in employees who are overtaxing themselves. Clearly, everyone needs to unplug at times. "Despite their multitasking abilities, there is a limit to how many inputs the millennials can focus on at once," says Eric Lesser, the global business services executive at IBM. "There must be a balance between speed and attention."

Some researchers are putting multitasking to the test. Frequent distractions from the main task at hand appeared to hurt productivity in a study at Microsoft. Researchers observed a group of workers at the software company and found that it took them 10 to 15 minutes to return to their ongoing tasks of writing reports or computer code after being interrupted by electronic messages.

No matter how young they are, millennials may have only so much capacity for multitasking. A study at the University of Oregon concluded that the human brain simply isn't designed for extreme multitasking and that the average person can focus on only a few things at once. In laboratory experiments with young adults ranging in age from 18 to 30, professors found that the subjects could hold only four items in their active memory.

Another experiment even casts doubt on whether young people are more adept multitaskers than their elders. The Institute for the Future of the Mind at the University of Oxford tested the impact of interruptions from communication devices on mental performance. A group of 18- to 21-year-olds and a group of 35- to 39-year-olds were asked to perform a task that required a high level of concentration. The younger group did better when there was no interruption. But when the subjects were interrupted by a phone call, text message to a cell phone, or an instant message on a computer, the younger group lost its advantage over the older group, which wasn't fazed much by the intrusion.

An even more pressing question is whether technology overload and excessive multitasking are taking a toll on reading and writing skills. It's becoming an increasingly serious issue as more college professors find that millennials resist reading full-length books because the tomes require too much sustained attention. In the face of such objections, some teachers are surrendering and assigning brief excerpts from books and short stories or articles. But many millennials don't even read short magazine and newspaper articles, preferring quick bits of information from the Internet instead. Some millennials also are playing video games rather than reading. Ironically, public libraries may be fueling that unfortunate trend by buying video games for young people to check out instead of books.

In a 2007 report, the National Endowment for the Arts concluded that Americans are spending less time reading and that reading comprehension skills are eroding. Millennials, in particular, are reading less than older adults. The report noted that the percentage of 18- to 24-year olds reading literature fell to 43% in 2002 from 60% in 1982.

The millennials' aversion to serious reading likely plays a part in its inferior writing skills. Employers are finding that this e-literate generation is barely literate in other forms of communication. They complain vehemently about young people's inability to compose a coherent, well-written memo. They find that millennials' writing is riddled with punctuation, grammar, and spelling errors, and it often lacks clarity, proper sentence structure, and logical organization. When trying to write persuasively, this generation is often at a loss to provide compelling arguments to support their thesis.

Employers gave millennials low marks for communication skills in a 2006 study titled "Are They Really Ready to Work?" that was produced by the Conference Board, Partnership for 21st Century Skills, Corporate Voices for Working Families, and the Society for Human Resource Management. About 47% of the respondents rated graduates of two-year colleges as deficient in grammar and spelling and in writing memos, letters, and technical reports clearly and effectively. Slightly more than a quarter rated graduates of four-year colleges deficient in those areas. Not surprisingly, the employers awarded millennials in both two-year and four-year colleges the highest grades for information technology skills.

Colleges and employers blame teachers for neglecting to develop basic writing skills starting in elementary school, but they also see technology's insidious influence at work, too. "It seems that their communication has suffered as a result of having been brought up in a world of e-mail and text messaging where it's so much less formal and totally acceptable to abbreviate not only words but also concepts and ideas," says Bruce Moore, associate director of the career management center at the Cox School of Business at Southern Methodist University. "Thus, their cover letters and other correspondence are relatively flat and lacking in personality and warmth."

Teachers and employers find it especially maddening when the shorthand digital language of the millennial generation carries over to academic and business writing. Young people sometimes go so far as to use the numerals 2 and 4 in place of the words "to" and "for" in formal writing. In a survey by the Pew Research Center and the College Board's National Commission on Writing, half of the teenagers said they sometimes omit proper punctuation marks and capitalization in schoolwork; more than one-third use text shortcuts, such as LOL for "laugh out loud"; and 25% insert smiley face symbols and other emoticons.

Ernst & Young even gives its text-challenged managers a helpful reference guide for translating cryptic millennial shorthand into intelligible words. Now the accounting firm's managers have no excuse for not recognizing that FBM means "fine by me" and that XLNT is short for "excellent." (See the accompanying table for more text translations.)

Deciphering Text Messages

Text	Translation
AISB	As it should be
BFF	Best friend forever
BLNT	Better luck next time
BM&Y	Between me and you
OMG	Oh my god
BRB	Be right back
CRBT	Crying really big tears
CWYL	Chat with you later
CYO	Catch you online
EG	Evil grin
FBM	Fine by me
FOMC	Falling off my chair
GOI	Get over it
IB	I'm back
JP	Just playing
KPC	Keeping parents clueless
NBD	No big deal
P911	Parents coming into room alert
PZ	Peace
RME	Rolling my eyes
RL	Real life
TKOY	Take care of yourself
UCMU	You crack me up
WE	Whatever
WU?	What's up?
XLNT	Excellent
YGG	You go girl

Alison Brod, president and founder of a public relations and marketing agency in New York City, is puzzled by her young employees' abominable writing, given the top high schools and colleges that many have attended. "Eighty percent of the e-mails I get, with no exaggeration, have spelling or grammar errors from this group," she says. "No one knows the difference between 'its' and 'it's' or 'stationery' and 'stationary.' They capitalize in strange places within a sentence, and I have yet to meet one who knows how to do a proper outline." She once received a thank-you e-mail from an interviewee who couldn't be bothered to press the shift key. The e-mail contained such lines as "i enjoyed meeting you," and ruined any chances for a job offer.

Even worse, Brod says, millennials aren't the least bit embarrassed or apologetic. "They will tell me that they just don't understand contractions," she says. "If they get a proper noun wrong, rather than Google a name or state, their attitude is that it just doesn't matter, that it's close enough."

Besides developing bad habits from texting and instant messaging, millennials also rely too much on computer programs for checking their spelling and grammar. Before hiring millennials, recruiters should ask them to write an essay or memo by hand without any opportunity to make computer software checks.

John Challenger, CEO of the outplacement firm Challenger, Gray & Christmas, advises college students to enroll in more business and technical writing courses, as well as creative writing and journalism classes. "History courses will also help students hone their writing skills, not to mention their critical thinking skills," he says. "Shortened syntax, incomplete sentences, and no punctuation may be acceptable for instant messaging between friends, but most offices require a much higher level of sophistication, even in e-mails between coworkers." His firm surveyed human resource executives and found that nearly half believe that entry-level job seekers lack adequate written communication abilities; more than a quarter also believe they need stronger critical thinking, interpersonal, and conflict-management skills.

Indeed, some educators and employers worry that the millennials' obsession with technology is robbing this generation of important interpersonal interactions and the development of social skills. Millennials usually prefer instant messaging to telephoning someone or walking over to a colleague's desk or a supervisor's office for a brief chat. But in such voice or face-to-face contacts, they would likely develop better listening and negotiation skills and stronger personal connections with their colleagues. Physical interactions also provide richer communication experiences as people read each other's body language and facial expressions.

Employers complain that they often must compete to get the attention of multitasking millennials, who aren't the best listeners, especially when they are plugged into iPods or other personal music players. In fact, there is clearly a generational conflict over iPods. Many managers consider them a sign of disrespect as well as inattentiveness. They say they have had to lay down the law and ban iPods from presentations, conferences, and other meetings.

Millennials insist that they can concentrate and multitask better listening to music or podcasts, but some managers believe they prevent employees from hearing what's going on around them. In reaction to their supervisors' griping, some millennials work with only one ear bud plugged in so that they aren't too isolated from the office environment.

According to a survey by the recruiting firm Spherion Corp., nearly half of adults age 25 to 29 listen to their personal music devices while working. That's the highest usage rate of any age group. Spherion advises employers to set ground rules, such as asking people to keep the volume low, designating certain areas of the workplace for listening, and developing polices for downloading music and other files on company computers.

Just the sight of iPods can rattle some managers. "Seeing our young workers listening to iPods while they're writing drives me nuts," says Kate Cronin, managing director of the New York City office of Ogilvy Public Relations Worldwide. "I would find it too distracting myself, but I have to say that their work is usually quite good even when they write a press release with an iPod connected to their ears. I have to assume that they're simply able to multitask in a way that I can't."

As with everything, there's a happy medium for multitasking and technology. Millennials need to slow down and unplug from time to time. They need to take a break from technology to relax, reflect, read, and interact with real people, not just the virtual world. Even fans of multitasking advise moderation. Matthew Schuyler, the human resources chief at Capital One, smiles when he sees young employees whip out their laptops and BlackBerries while they're waiting in line to pay for their lunches at the company cafeteria. "Multitasking means more productivity, but we have to be careful not to burn people out, to make sure they take downtime," he says. "We include in our corporate training some discussion of taking time out for weekends or vacations. BlackBerries are called CrackBerries for a reason, you know."

CHAPTER HIGHLIGHTS

- The millennial generation is the most technology savvy group of young people in history. They thrive on multitasking and social networking, whether at home, in the classroom, or at work.

- To hold the attention of easily distracted millennials, schools and colleges are making learning a multimedia experience by incorporating podcasts, videos, computer games, and other interactive technologies into their lessons. Yet they also have to be vigilant to prevent millennial students from misusing computers, cell phones, and other devices for personal entertainment or even cheating in the classroom.

- More companies are realizing that to compete for talent they must satisfy the millennial generation's demands for such tools as instant messaging, social networking, blogs, wikis, and corporate training podcasts. Some employers, however, still ban instant messages and videos from the workplace because of concerns about lower productivity and potential security and technical problems.

- The millennial generation is unusually uninhibited on social networks and other Web sites. That presents an opportunity for some companies to check out job candidates on the Internet and weed out those who might be troublesome. But employers also must be cautious and remind millennials not to use company laptops, BlackBerries, and other technology gear for personal gossip.

- Multitasking may increase millennials' efficiency on many projects, but it can undermine concentration and performance on more complex tasks. Companies should be watchful for excessive multitasking and tell millennials to slow down and take a break from technology.

- College professors and corporate recruiters are concerned that technology is damaging the millennial generation's writing abilities and interpersonal communication skills. E-mail and text messages have certainly contributed to the generation's sloppy writing, and their preference for interacting virtually is reducing the amount of valuable face-to-face interaction in the workplace.

8

Free to
Be Me

Tyler Shaw felt trapped in "meeting hell." He had just joined a new team at Best Buy Co. and was horrified to find that he was expected to spend five hours each week in meetings without any set agendas. To Shaw, it was the ultimate example of inefficiency and an obstacle to his goal of achieving a pleasing balance between his job and his personal life. "All of those meetings were as painful to me as kryptonite is to Superman," he says.

Shaw quickly started campaigning against so many meetings, questioning what they accomplished. "People are so used to shuffling into a conference room like sheep, thinking that if they're all in a room together, they'll get something done," he says. "It's a hard habit to break, and I got some flak from other people for trying to cut back on so many time-wasting meetings. But we did end up cutting out a lot of them."

A member of the millennial generation, Shaw doesn't believe in sacrificing his personal life for unproductive meetings and inefficiency on the job. A senior manager for digital services, he is part of a program at the electronics retailer called Results-Only Work Environment, or ROWE for short. He can set his own work hours and decide whether to stay at home or go into the office, as long as he gets the job done on time. ROWE puts the onus on the employee to figure out the best schedule and strategy for satisfying the company's expectations.

Before he moved to the corporate office and the ROWE program, Shaw provided computer services as a member of Best Buy's Geek Squad and managed to balance work and play in that job, too. "I would line up almost twice as many computers as other technicians and fix them really quickly," he recalls. "When I was at work, I was focused and driven. My goal was to get as much done as possible so I could go jogging or play video games. The system worked well there, since we had clear goals and metrics upon which we were measured. I could easily say, I have done my part, and go home."

In his corporate job, his goals and schedules aren't quite so clear-cut. If he's slow and inefficient, Shaw pays the price with long hours slaving at his computer. But if he works hard and smart, he achieves the flexibility that makes him feel happy and empowered. "I do my best work when I am rested, when I eat breakfast and lunch, work out regularly, spend time with my family, and play video games occasionally to recharge," he says. "I just see so many people running ragged; they work hard, but too much and not at 100 percent."

This is how Shaw describes his typical workday. The time he awakens at his home in Golden Valley, Minnesota, depends on the work that needs to be done that day. While still in bed, he reads e-mail on his smartphone, scans the latest news, and reviews his schedule. Throughout the day, he checks e-mail on his phone rather than tether himself to his computers at home or at Best Buy. Sometimes he attends meetings from his home office via a teleconference, but he will drive into Best Buy if the meetings are with a larger, cross-functional group of employees. If there's a long enough break between meetings, he heads to the gym and works out for an hour and a half, then showers and either goes home or to another meeting at the office. When he returns home, he helps care for his baby boy and keeps checking e-mail. He might play some video games or go shopping with his wife. If he's feeling anxious about something at the office, he may do a little extra work at home in the evening to feel more comfortable about going in the next day.

When Shaw does have to make an appearance at Best Buy's offices, he tries to time his trip to miss heavy traffic. "In a ROWE environment, every minute counts, and I do not want to spend it in traffic," he says. "I find I get more done at home since I control the environment. I can close my office door and just dive into work. I often find two or three hours at home can equal a day at the office with all the interruptions."

With the arrival of millions of millennials in the workplace, traditional work patterns may never be the same. Millennials like Shaw intend to become agents of change, pushing flexibility to the top of the workplace agenda. Although baby boomers and generation Xers negotiated some flexible work arrangements in recent years, they weren't as intensely committed to achieving a balanced life as the millennials are.

"Young people today are much more willing to express the importance of work-life balance," says John Ventola, cochairman of the hiring committee and summer program at the law firm Choate, Hall & Stewart in Boston. "It was important to me, too, but I didn't have the courage to talk about it." He finds that most law school graduates understand that the firm's clients come first, but some expect flexibility no matter what the business demands may be. "We do our best to accommodate people, but we still need to get the job done," Ventola says. "Some students and junior associates react to that as unfair; they don't get it that this is a business."

Choate will no doubt encounter many more such demanding law students. Millennials view work-life balance as their right. And they want the whole shebang: flextime, compressed work weeks, telecommuting, home offices, job sharing, part-time options, maternity and paternity leave, and occasional sabbaticals. Besides flexibility, millennials also prefer a more casual work environment and relaxed dress code that allow them to be themselves and feel comfortable. Some millennials even believe that the workplace should be fun and entertaining.

"We have to answer some tough questions about how much people are going to have to work and what the workplace should be like for them," says W. Stanton Smith, national director of Next Generation Initiatives at the accounting firm Deloitte & Touche. "Millennials especially want to know about flexibility later in their careers when they have families."

In a 2007 *Wall Street Journal*/Harris Interactive survey, more than 70% of M.B.A. recruiters said they increasingly find that job candidates are seeking positions offering them benefits for balancing work-life issues. Whereas traditionally it was female baby boomers and gen Xers who sought flexible work arrangements to help them care for children, there isn't a very big gender split on the importance of work-life harmony with the millennial generation. In Universum's annual survey of M.B.A. graduates, more than half of all respondents now list career-life balance as their primary goal, up from 44% in 2004. About 57% of women put it first, compared with 48% of men.

What millennials want most is control over their lives. Face time is an alien concept to this generation. They abhor clocks and fixed schedules. Although millennials need structure and clear directions for their projects and other assignments, they want to be able to perform that work where they like and when they like. "The big revelation for us about millennials is how they view work," says Kaye Foster-Cheek, vice president for human resources at Johnson & Johnson. "For this generation, work is not a place you go; work is a thing you do."

Companies should realize that millennials will head for the door if employers refuse to provide reasonable working hours and conditions. Millennials watched workaholic parents who gave their all for employers and then lost jobs in corporate downsizings. So much for 60-hour work weeks and unwavering loyalty. "Millennials actually mean it when they talk about work-life balance," says Seth Dunn, a manager and recruiter for General Electric Co. "This is not a generation we should expect to stay in the office doing noncritical work on weekends."

Technology, of course, will play a big part in freeing millennials from a rigid work schedule. Millennials are expert at multitasking and making the most of the technology that gives them access to e-mail and corporate intranets from virtually anywhere. The millennial generation's attitude: Why stay at the office until five if I want to go to my kid's soccer game? Just text me on my cell phone if you need me.

Many millennials see their careers and personal life as one. They don't talk about balancing work and life but rather about blending them. They want to break down boundaries between work and play—take the afternoon off to play tennis and resume working late in the evening after the kids are tucked in. "Millennials want a life where work and life activities intermingle throughout the day," says Dennis Garritan, director of graduate programs in human resource management at New York University. "The message I get from millennials, is 'Yes, I'll work for you, but I need to bring my pet parrot to work, and by the way, where's the cappuccino machine?'"

Employers have eliminated some of the divisions between work and personal life by providing on-site fitness centers, child-care facilities, banks, movie rentals, bakeries, and concierges to make dinner or vacation reservations. Google Inc. has created the ultimate merged environment of work and personal life at its Mountain View, California, Googleplex headquarters, with its gourmet meals, oil changes, car washes, massage therapy, hair stylists, gym, dry cleaner, and bike repair shop. There is even an on-site doctor.

But blurring the lines between work and home also can be stressful. If millennials bring too much of their personal lives into the office, the workday will become continuous, without a start or finish. They won't enjoy the relaxation and refreshment that come from fully escaping the workplace.

Millennials maintain that they "work to live," unlike older generations that have "lived to work." No doubt millennials want lucrative compensation, but they also want time to spend it. They want time for family and for their personal goals and interests—even if it means taking unpaid days off or buying extra vacation time. "I am certainly willing to take a pay cut if I can get more vacation time, because work-life balance is extremely important to me," says Dania Stotts, who was studying for her M.B.A. degree in 2008 at the University of California at Davis. "One of my main concerns as I reenter the workplace after my degree will be whether it will be culturally acceptable in my organization to use all of my vacation time."

Some employers are getting in tune with Stotts and other millennials by offering extended breaks from work. Stotts might like the management consulting firm Oliver Wyman, which lets employees work only 10 or 11 months of the year at a reduced salary and offers them sabbaticals of up to six months. Employees have taken time off for everything from producing movies for the Montreal World Film Festival to playing for the Edmonton Eskimos football club. "This generation wants to progress professionally, but they do not want to give up on passions that may be outside of their core career focus," says Matthew Bennett, director of global recruiting for Oliver Wyman. "Chances are they will stay with us longer if they can take a few months off to follow their dreams."

FLEXIBLE FIRMS

Can millennials really find the flexibility and freedom they so long for? It is certainly possible, but the search for the right fit could take time.

Although there has been a move toward workplace flexibility over the past two decades, the results have been spotty and slow in coming. Sure, many companies now allow a few people to work from home. Some also have made Friday hours flexible. But the majority of employees still report most days to the same location and put in at least eight hours there. So millennials will have to pick their employers with care.

Hewitt Associates, a human resources consulting firm, reports that 88% of employers offer alternative work arrangements to at least some employees. Most common (78%) is part-time employment. But that isn't what millennials are most interested in. They primarily want flexibility in full-time jobs. According to Hewitt, roughly 60% of companies offer at least some employees a form of flextime. A little more than a third let some people work at home and telecommute. In addition, about a quarter make job sharing and compressed work schedules available.

A few companies—Best Buy, International Business Machines Corp., and Capital One Financial Corp.—are setting the bar high, embracing flexibility and mobile work patterns in a big way. The ROWE program that Tyler Shaw works in seems tailor-made for the millennial generation because it measures performance by the outcome, not by the clock. In this clockless culture, employees can do their jobs from anywhere, and they need not toil alone when they're working out of Best Buy's office building. Some Best Buy teams still get together, just not in conference rooms. Instead, they congregate at each other's homes or at coffee shops. After making progress on a project, they all might take in a movie together or play Frisbee golf.

For flexible work styles to succeed, it takes a strong commitment to change, a risk-taking mentality, and perhaps most important of all, trust in the employees. "Managers have to let their guard down and get over the mindset that their employees need to be here at our corporate campus from nine to five," says Kristina Parker, who heads up recruiting at Best Buy. About three-quarters of Best Buy's corporate headquarters staff are now part of the ROWE program. The company plans to test it in some stores, but flexibility won't be as easily achieved on the selling floor as in office cubicles.

Even at Best Buy headquarters, Shaw acknowledges, ROWE still isn't universally accepted. For some managers, it's too radical a change. "There are some people who feel hostile about ROWE and want to continue to micromanage," Shaw says. "Sometimes I'll hear a snide comment from someone when I come into the office at 11 in the morning."

Shaw encourages doubting colleagues to view the ROWE system from an economic perspective. "People spend their time like money, and time has power because it is a limited, nonrenewable resource," he says. "The arbitrary rules we enforce on each other are essentially like price controls and tariffs that disrupt the market. ROWE is in essence a free-market system— no controls, no tariffs. People spend their time in the most efficient manner possible to get the desired outcome."

At IBM, mobile workers may soon outnumber deskbound employees. Already, about 40% of IBM employees work virtually—from home, client offices, the road, or a "mobility center" where they can drop in to use phones and Internet connections. "We offer millennials true work-life integration," says Karen Calo, IBM's vice president for global talent. "People can do work anyplace anytime. They are not judged on their face time."

Rick Genett, the marketing manager for WebSphere Commerce, considers IBM's flexible work options "priceless." When he and his wife lived in Manhattan, he could spend two or three days working from home and the company's offices in New York City. That arrangement saved him an hour and a half commute to IBM's Armonk, New York, offices.

He also can avoid late nights at the office working on global projects. When he led an international work group with members scattered in distant time zones in Australia, India, and Japan, he could connect with them online and by phone from home after eating dinner with his wife. "The setup took a situation that would have had a large personal-life impact for someone who was newly married and really minimized it to nothing," he says.

Now, Genett has moved to White Plains, New York, much closer to Armonk, but he still has the flexibility to leave in the early afternoon to work on group projects for a part-time M.B.A. program he has enrolled in. "I head down to campus and work remotely without missing a beat," he says. "Again, a win-win for both myself and IBM."

The workforce at Capital One is also being freed from the traditional cubicle culture. The company's "Future of Work" strategy not only allows people to work remotely from home or the road but also opens up office space for greater mobility and collaboration. "We used to have a lot of caves and cube farms, but now there are minimal walls and maximum open space and technology," says Matthew Schuyler, the chief human resources officer. "You can meet with your team in one corner of the building for an hour, then go upstairs and camp out with your laptop and BlackBerry to work alone." The phone system has been redesigned so that employees can activate their personal numbers at any work station, and "quiet zones" and "huddle rooms" have been set aside for private conversations and focused individual work.

Such informal, nontraditional offices are exactly what millennials crave as their jobs become more flexible and mobile, according to a research report by Steelcase Inc., the office furniture maker. The study concluded that millennials consider the ideal workspace to be "fun, open, and collaborative" with "flexible, fluid space and work stations, personalized work-station design, visual displays everywhere, and a plug 'n play, wireless tech environment."

Beyond appealing to millennials, the open, mobile workplace also is a financial boon. Schuyler says Capital One has saved "millions of dollars" in real estate costs with so much shared workspace. For example, 1,500 people are now assigned to a building in Richmond, Virginia, that once held only 600. There isn't an overcrowding problem because only about one-third of those 1,500 employees show up on any given day.

CAVEAT EMPTOR

Unfortunately, work-life balance is sometimes merely a millennial mirage. This generation should beware of blanket promises of a balanced life, because they may turn out to be more hype than substance. You might be free to do your job wherever and whenever you like, but if there's a mountain of work to get done, that hardly means balance.

Seniority may also be a limiting factor. Recruiting brochures and Web sites promising flexibility may mislead millennials into believing they can be a mobile worker, whether from home or the beach, from their first day on the job. Although companies may well provide flexible options, they may be available only to a small cadre of experienced employees. Some managers feel that they lack control over their remote employees and can't count on them to be productive. They would be especially reluctant to let entry-level millennials out of their sight for long. That often means a rude awakening when millennials show up for work.

Millennials also should not let themselves be fooled into thinking that flexible work is possible in every job in every industry. Companies may be able to offer millennials flexible work options in some white-collar office positions, but some jobs simply don't lend themselves to work-life balance.

Millennials' strong desire for flexibility is a significant challenge for Union Pacific Corp. as it tries to hire more young people to replace retirees. Many railroad workers must be ready to report for duty on short notice, whether at night, on weekends and holidays, or in the worst possible weather. "That's a challenging lifestyle for anyone, but it's especially misaligned with the millennial generation's desire for work-life balance," says Roy Schroer, assistant vice president for recruitment.

Unionized employees must build up seniority to be eligible for more regular schedules, but millennials aren't patient enough to wait it out. For Schroer, that translates into a major retention problem. "Millennials are not interested in paying their dues and earning what seniority gets you in terms of schedules," he says. "They don't want to be at the beck and call of any company for very long. They want to know how quickly they can get the plum opportunities."

Millennials may not like what they hear, but honesty is definitely the best policy. If they hope to retain new recruits, employers must be quite frank up front about how much flexibility to expect. For example, PricewaterhouseCoopers tries not to delude prospective recruits on its college careers Web page. The accounting firm bluntly states, "Your needs for flexibility require communication and agreement with team members. Our business is serving clients. Client demands can limit flexibility. Work-life is measured in the long-term, not the short-term."

As Ernst & Young recruiters field more and more questions from students about work-life balance, they also are trying to paint a realistic picture. They, of course, tout the company's commitment to flexible hours, reduced schedules, telecommuting, and parental leave. But Dan Black, director of Americas campus recruiting, says it's important that students also understand that there's a "breaking-in period" for newbies. "We won't allow brand-new staff to come and go as they please," he adds, "because they don't know enough yet to prioritize their time."

The accounting firm conveys to millennials that it's a two-way street. "We do allow this generation to manage its life from day one," Black says. "If they have a wedding or dentist's appointment, we absolutely will not make work more important than personal health or major obligations. But because they're in client services, I let students know that work will infringe on their lives sometimes." As a long-term employee, he tells new recruits that he has found his own personal balance by not spending weekends in the office but by doing work at home some nights after his children are asleep.

Even when flexible work schedules become available, some employees will struggle to manage them successfully. Well aware of the complexities, Ernst & Young has created a Web site devoted to tips on making a flexible schedule work. It offers pointers on how to manage a virtual team, how to deal with client and team expectations when working a reduced schedule, and how to use technology to enhance flexibility.

ZIGZAGGING CAREERS

Work-life balance may slow your momentum, but it doesn't have to bring your career to a dead stop. More companies are redefining their career development process to allow for more variety in how employees navigate the organization. The route need not always be a straight line any longer. Workers can zigzag up, across, down, and up again. They can detour to an "off ramp" for a while and then return via an "on ramp" that takes them to the same or a lower spot in the organization.

Some employers tell new recruits that how they split their time is up to them. The company provides flexibility, but the employees control the throttle on how hard they work. They're going to have to put in long hours and travel if they're aiming for senior management. But there's also room for people who want to strike a better balance between work and personal life.

Some law firms are becoming more flexible about billable hours so as to give young associates a choice in how intensely they work. Perkins Coie, a Seattle-based law firm, will let associates reduce their annual billable-hour requirements from 2,000 to 1,800 or 1,900. Should they exceed their new lower level, they will receive a bonus. "Some of our young associates want more freedom after work than they could have if they billed 2,200 or 2,300 hours a year," says Darrin Emerick, director of personnel. "Retention is definitely a challenge, so we need to make the workplace as appealing as possible. It can easily cost a couple hundred thousand dollars to replace an associate."

In an online survey of law firm associates, the American Bar Association's *ABA Journal* found that 84% of respondents would accept a pay cut in exchange for lower billable-hour requirements. Skeptics question whether associates will look like slackers and take themselves out of the running for a partnership if they shoot for a lower billable-hour target. Still, many law school students believe a saner life is more important than money and titles. "We kept hearing from friends that they're pretty miserable with 18-hour days six or seven days a week," says Andrew Bruck, copresident of Building a Better Legal Profession, a student-driven grassroots organization that is publicizing law firms' billable-hour requirements, diversity hiring records, and pro bono work. "We're trying to improve the quality of life at law firms. There's a pretty high depression rate among young attorneys."

Bruck, who attended law school at Stanford University, notes that work-life balance is "like the elephant in the room" during job interviews. "Students don't want to bring it up for fear that it will look like they're lazy, and it's hard to know what's true from the law firms' slick recruiting materials," he says. "So the burden should be on the firms to explain in detail their policies on billable hours and flexibility."

Like lawyers, many management consultants and accountants also put in long hours at the expense of their personal lives. Although consulting and accounting firms can't suddenly put everyone on a 40-hour workweek, some are giving employees alternatives that let them slow down, at least for a while. Boston Consulting Group Inc. is offering employees more unpaid leaves of absence and part-time schedules, as well as greater career-track variety. When a consultant with a few years of experience needs more time at home and less intensity at work, for example, he can "roll off" the consulting track and switch to an administrative job.

The firm is also experimenting with flexible promotion timing. "We are an up-or-out environment, but we want to ensure more flexibility and promote when employees are really ready," says Dorota Keverian, global director of consultant human resources. "People who get off track for a while may need more time, and a Ph.D. candidate may not be on the same timeline as an M.B.A. recruit."

Millennials, however, may be reluctant to take advantage of Boston Consulting's menu of flexibility options. Many consultants have been loath to take leaves of absence because they fear being left in the dust by type-A colleagues. "Where leaves of absence are more accepted, they're being taken by more people," Keverian says. "The take-up rate is higher in Germany, for example, than in the United States."

At Deloitte & Touche, the buzzword these days is "mass career customization." That's a mouthful, but it boils down to adjusting the speed and direction of your career to fit your changing life. Deloitte is gradually rolling out the career planning program to employees, who will move on "lattices" instead of ladders as they maneuver through their careers. They can climb, take lateral moves, or make planned descents. "Young people are telling us they need the flexibility to fade in and out of work," says Cathleen Benko, vice chairman and chief talent officer. "With mass career customization, we are looking for alternatives to the one-size-fits-all approach to the proverbial corporate ladder."

Millennials sometimes believe that reaching a senior level such as executive vice president or managing partner means giving up a personal life altogether. The top dogs look like workaholics, and many millennials will leave the company rather than face that kind of future. To retain and groom millennials for senior management, companies will have to demonstrate convincingly that even the CEO has a life outside the office and can achieve some balance between work and play. That means bosses should be role models for work-life balance.

To that end, Deloitte has created a new initiative called "Compulsively Transparent." It aims to demonstrate that flexibility is truly part of its corporate culture from the lowest to highest levels of the organization. Rather than pretend that work always comes first, the firm is encouraging managers and executives to be honest about the times they duck out of work early to coach their kid's baseball team or get a haircut and manicure. Benko took the lead in pushing Compulsively Transparent, announcing to a roomful of Deloitte's "big guns" that she had skipped a high-level meeting to go shopping at a major sale at the Nordstrom department store. "Younger people don't want to be like they perceive us to be," she says. "But we can send a huge signal to them by our example, by not making excuses when we fit life into work."

EXPRESS YOURSELF

In their quest for workplace balance, millennials also seek freedom to express themselves personally. They want more than casual Fridays. They want casual everyday.

But millennials are clashing with some tradition-bound companies over their wardrobes, tattoos, body piercings, and rainbow-hued hair. Some managers cringe when they see young employees sashay into the office wearing torn jeans and flip-flops and sporting tattoos on their arms and piercings on their face. One young woman at an investment bank told me she'd be willing to pay $20 a day for the chance to wear jeans to work. But so far, no one has taken her up on her offer.

Some employers may have no choice but to become more tolerant. According to a survey by the Pew Research Center in Washington, DC, 36% of 18- to 25-year-olds have a tattoo, 25% have dyed their hair an untraditional color, and 30% have a piercing somewhere other than their earlobe. Tattoos are so popular these days that even the U.S. Army relaxed its policies to avoid losing qualified recruits. Tattoos now are permitted on the hands and back of the neck, assuming they aren't "extremist, indecent, sexist, or racist." But the Army stresses that tattoos still are forbidden on soldiers' heads and faces.

As for apparel, millennials should enjoy some degree of freedom. Hewitt Associates, the human resources consulting firm, found that 58% of employers allow casual dress on a regular basis; 10% go casual only on Fridays. But "casual" is in the eye of the beholder. Johnson & Johnson defines casual as chinos and polo shirts, for example, whereas T-shirts and shorts would be the casual look at some technology companies. KPMG, which permits business casual dress that isn't sloppy, is letting millennials know just how far they can go in expressing their sartorial individuality. In the accounting firm's recruiting magazine for college students, KPMG details what's appropriate and what isn't. Some tips: "If it's too tight, it ain't right," "The bling? Not something to bring to the office," and for casual Friday jeans, "no holes, tears, sequins, embroidery, appliqués, or fringe." The bottom line at KPMG: "It's always better to be overdressed than underdressed."

For a financial services company, Capital One is unusually accommodating when it comes to office wardrobe. Ties are required for meetings with customers and vendors, but otherwise it's a personal choice. In some offices, especially in warmer climates, it isn't unusual to see employees clad in shorts and T-shirts. "We don't spend our time fussing over it," says Matthew Schuyler, the human resources chief. "You should be comfortable at work, but you have to do it within reasonable boundaries or you'll be challenged by your fellow employees. Our philosophy is that we hire intelligent people who can decide if wearing blue jeans every day is okay."

Gretchen Neels, a Boston-based consultant, believes that companies must understand that millennials' flip-flops and jeans are an integral part of their identity. "They're all caught up in how they project themselves to the world," she says. To avoid workplace warfare, she advises employers to spell out wardrobe and appearance standards very clearly and then stand their ground. "No spandex, no yoga clothing, shoes must be worn in the office, and by the way, socks are not considered shoes," she suggests managers tell their millennial hires. "Also, be sure to explain the why. Tell them that clients not only want to know you're worth the rates they are paying; they want you to look like you're worth it, as well."

That's the attitude of Alison Brod. As president and founder of a public relations and marketing agency in New York City, Brod enforces a rule that jeans are forbidden at client meetings. When her millennial employees protest that client representatives sometime wear jeans themselves, she replies, "That is fine, but they pay for an image when they pay for a PR agency." For client meetings, she also must remind them to apply some makeup and ditch the chewing gum. "Many of these women believe that comfort trumps all," she says. "They are an attractive group and feel that they look great in jeans without makeup, but don't realize that looking hot doesn't mean it looks professional."

Workplace attire clearly remains a contentious issue, judging from the spirited feedback to a *Wall Street Journal* article about young people dressing down at law firms in jeans and Ugg boots. "If the job is done with precision, then who cares? A moron in a suit is still a moron," a supporter of casual dress commented on the newspaper's Law Blog. Another reader offered this suggestion: "Hey, partners, let us work from home and you won't have to worry about seeing us in cotton pants, golf shirts, or Uggs."

Opposing counsel offered these comments:

"If big law firms didn't treat Harvard and other top law school grads like they were gods, they probably wouldn't be so narcissistic and feel so entitled to wear yoga outfits, Uggs, jeans, and khakis to work."

"Companies have a wide range of choice in firms these days, and they want counsel that looks and acts the part. Quirky and individualistic is fine, just not sloppy and too casual. Also, wash your hair, wear some makeup if you are a woman, and make sure your nails are clean."

ARE WE HAVING FUN YET?

Millennials just want to have fun—at work. That may sound like heresy to managers, but this generation detests nothing as much as drudgery and boredom. "They look at the work-place as a social organization, not just a job," one corporate recruiter told me.

Although "fun" may be not be in the vocabulary of most employers, some firms are adding a bit of frivolity to the workday to keep millennials happy. Just as it provides employees lots of services for taking care of personal chores, Google also has earned a reputation for its playful workplace atmosphere, from the baby grand piano to pool tables and big exercise balls to roller hockey in the parking lot.

Not many companies can compete with Google's allure, but the Seattle law firm Perkins Coie is proud of its "happiness committee." The committee surprises lawyers and their staffs with bags of candy, milk shakes, and other treats. In some offices, employees get flowers on their desks on May Day, while others celebrate Chinese New Year and Mardi Gras.

In a similar vein, Deloitte has created what it calls the Office of Surprise. There isn't really a physical office, but the firm has started coming up with entertaining programs and such unexpected perks as four extra days off in the summer. One of its first projects was the "What's Your Deloitte?" Film Festival. Given the explosive growth of YouTube and video creation on cell phones and handheld cameras, Deloitte feels that encouraging self-expression through film and other media is now essential in recruiting and retaining millennials. For the competition, Deloitte provided video cameras to employees, who ended up sharing their impressions of the firm in more than 370 films. The winning videos were posted on YouTube.

Some companies are helping young employees find opportunities to socialize together both at work and after hours. Such activities build camaraderie as employees get better acquainted with each other and learn about common interests. Google offers ski trips, company movie days, summer picnics, and Halloween and holiday parties. At Ogilvy Public Relations Worldwide in New York City, the Take 5 Action Committee was formed to plan social activities, such as the holiday karaoke party, the build your own sundae bar, impromptu happy hours, and "name the caption" photo contests. "The millennial generation has a lot of expectations about getting promoted every year," says Kate Cronin, managing director of Ogilvy's New York office. "We're trying to create a collegial, enjoyable atmosphere, so they will still want to come to work even if they aren't promoted every year."

Harris Corp., a communications and information technology company in Melbourne, Florida, has developed a formal Graduate Acclimation and Development Program (GRAD) for new hires to help them make the transition from college to the workplace. Some young employees had taken to calling Melbourne "Melboring" because of the large number of retirees. GRAD's goal is to lure more millennials by providing social activities, such as kayaking, ice skating, and paintball, and community service projects, such as beach cleanups and Habitat for Humanity house-building projects.

Because some employees take smoking breaks outside, millennials also have petitioned Harris to give them "play breaks" by installing foosball and Ping-Pong tables. Cindy Kane, director of corporate relations at Harris, would be more than happy to oblige. "Because there's going to be a talent shortage, we need to be more flexible and adaptable to the millennial generation and its needs," she says. "This generation is going to rule the roost before long."

CHAPTER HIGHLIGHTS

- "Work-life balance" is the mantra of the millennial generation. Unlike any generation before them, millennials are demanding that companies give them flexible working conditions so that they can have time for family and personal passions.

- A few companies are attracting millennials with policies that let them work anywhere anytime as long as they get the job done. Their mobile employees use technology tools to effectively blend their jobs and personal lives.

- Some companies are making clear the limitations on flexible work arrangements, but many are not as explicit. So millennials should evaluate corporate promises of work-life balance with a skeptical eye. To their dismay, they may find that many flexible work options are available to only a small number of experienced employees.

- To achieve flexibility, millennials may need to rethink their career paths. Some companies are encouraging employees to take a nonlinear view of their careers and consider taking breaks from work, making lateral moves, and even accepting positions lower on the organizational chart to better suit their changing personal lives.

- Millennials want the freedom to express their individuality in a casual workplace environment. Although companies should become more tolerant of this generation's relaxed style of dressing and its tattoos and body piercings, they also need to establish some guidelines for appropriate attire, especially in meetings with customers and clients.

- Lighten up. The millennial generation expects the workplace to be fun. To retain their young employees, some companies are surprising them with sweet treats, bonus vacation days, and social outings.

9

Recruiting in Cyberspace

When most young people log on to YouTube, the hugely popular video-sharing Web site, they're apt to watch the new Mariah Carey music video, a popular skit from *Saturday Night Live*, or the latest scrappy political debate.

What they're seeking is entertainment, not a new job. But KPMG, the global auditing firm, hopes to change that. Now YouTube visitors also can look for a job by taking a peek at KPMG Go, a college recruiting channel developed expressly for the video-driven millennial generation. It may not be able to compete for attention with Mariah Carey and Barack Obama, but KPMG's YouTube channel is still a highly significant development that may well represent the future of college recruiting.

Companies must meet millennials on their own turf, and today that usually means not on campus but rather somewhere in cyberspace. What better place than YouTube, KPMG's recruiting managers figured. "We needed a fresh, new way to break through the clutter," says Shawn Quill, marketing account executive for campus recruiting. "In our focus groups with students, we found that YouTube was the most visited, most influential site. This generation grew up with video games and hundreds of cable TV channels; they expect to be entertained when they're being informed."

Videos on KPMG Go focus heavily on the personal experiences of both new and veteran employees. By presenting the career journeys of more seasoned employees, the firm aims to impress millennials with the message that they can build a long career filled with global opportunities.

In one of the short clips, an intern named Manny, who is starting his first day at KPMG in Shanghai, says he's excited about his new job because "I've spent enough time thinking global; it's time for action." But he adds that he also is feeling awfully hot in his business suit and tie on the streets of sweltering Shanghai. In another video clip, a managing partner talks about the firm's community service and his own involvement with the Boy Scouts of America in San Francisco.

The KPMG Go channel also links to a KPMG magazine for students and to the careers section of the firm's own Web site, which includes an interactive tool that matches college majors to different practices at the firm. Enter mathematics as your major, and the site informs you that you could do economic and valuation services or financial risk management.

KPMG Go wasn't exactly an overnight sensation with only about 12,000 channel views in its first few weeks. But as one of the first recruiters to try YouTube, KPMG expects awareness of its channel to increase steadily.

Like KPMG, more companies are realizing that they must go beyond formulaic recruiting techniques if they hope to generate any buzz with this generation of students. As competition for the most talented millennials has intensified, the old tried-and-true hiring strategies simply aren't working as well anymore. Merely inviting students to corporate presentations and cocktail parties won't command the attention of the tech-obsessed millennials. In fact, nearly two-thirds of the M.B.A. recruiters in a 2007 *Wall Street Journal*/Harris Interactive survey said that to attract top job candidates, they must resort to new tactics, ranging from searching online resume databases to joining social networking sites.

Beyond helping them reach millennials, innovative recruiting strategies can lend companies an image of being cool and on the cutting edge. International Business Machines Corp., which recruits at more than 100 U.S. universities, is planning to increase its online recruiting activities, particularly for its Extreme Blue internship program. For example, the company is setting up meeting spaces and islands in Second Life, a virtual community, for a variety of events, including coffee talks, recruiter question-and-answer sessions, educational lectures, and online interviews. Students would log on, create avatars to physically represent themselves, and then visit IBM Island. Senior business leaders, engineers, and inventors, who often can't travel to campuses and job fairs because of work demands, also would be able to participate in such virtual events. "Technology is part of the DNA of today's younger generation," says Karen Calo, IBM's vice president for global talent. "They're naturally attracted to things like Second Life and expect IBM as an innovative company to be there."

Of course, companies should realize that their recruiting pitches in cyberspace will not be accepted at face value. Millennials won't settle for the company line on corporate Web sites and social networking pages. They are avid information seekers and will scour the Internet for unfiltered opinions of potential employers. If millennials Google the name of most organizations, from KPMG to the U.S. Army, they are sure to find a plethora of critical news articles and blog postings. Run an Internet search of KPMG, for instance, and numerous references to its much-publicized tax shelter fraud scandal pop up. And an Army search turns up antiwar sites that question the military's performance in Iraq and show horrific images of Americans maimed in battle and prisoners abused by soldiers at the Abu Ghraib prison. Companies can't hide from publicity about negative events. But they can ensure that their online recruiting messages are credible, and they can assertively respond to inaccurate and reputation-damaging Internet gossip.

SOCIAL NETWORKING

More recruiters are seeing great potential in the Internet's social networks because they provide access to the places where thousands of millennials congregate virtually and communicate with their friends. Like KPMG, a small but growing number of companies already are experimenting with such sites as Facebook and YouTube in hopes of reeling in top talent. Others, however, are waiting to see if it's effective and if there's any backlash from millennials.

Making recruiting overtures on social sites is a touchy matter. Major recruiters, such as General Electric Co., are treading lightly because they fear they will offend millennials who want to keep their favorite networking sites purely social. Indeed, some young people may resent and ultimately reject companies that intrude with a recruiting pitch into what they consider their personal meeting places. That's why KPMG took a cautious approach with its YouTube channel and tried not to be overly promotional. "You don't want the same kind of videos that you show on your careers Web site," Quill says. "We wanted a lot of unedited, user-generated videos that our interns and young hires can relate to. You need to be authentic with this new generation."

Verizon Communications Inc. also decided to take a very soft sell approach when it started recruiting employees on Facebook. "Our goal is to target people we'd like to entice to join Verizon, but we certainly don't want to annoy anyone," says Odesa Stapleton, director of talent management. "We're not saying go buy our phones; we're just saying if you are interested in a career with us, then here's some information and a link to our Web site." Verizon can target people on Facebook who attended a particular college or majored in a certain field, such as engineering or finance. In addition, Verizon enlists its own employees with Facebook pages to invite their friends on the social network to apply for jobs at the telecommunications company.

Ernst & Young, the big accounting firm, realized Facebook's potential early on and established a recruiting page on the site in 2006. The firm tries to allay any fears that it is on Facebook to snoop around people's profiles. It states on its Facebook page, "We are not interested in seeing your profiles. It's not that we're not interested in you, but we respect your privacy and understand that you use Facebook to socialize with your friends. Joining the EY Careers group does not allow anyone to see your profile who didn't already have access to it." (Of course, many other employers are checking out the Facebook and MySpace profiles of prospective hires and nixing those with salacious content. Sage advice to millennials: clean up your social networking pages before applying for jobs.)

To keep people coming back, Ernst & Young updates its Facebook page weekly with new content and pictures. Much of the page is promotional, of course, with photos of happy workers and gushy comments from summer interns. The most provocative part of the page is the Wall, a message board for visitors. Most of the posts are requests for information about internships and replies from the firm's recruiters. Some people make fawning comments about E&Y to try to ingratiate themselves with the firm. Others remark about random things such as a lunar eclipse or send flippant messages like this one: "Dear Ernst and Young, I just did my tax return for the first time. Can I please have a job?"

But most visitors to the recruiting page are quite serious about landing a position at E&Y. Some anxious applicants go to the Wall, fearful that they didn't get hired. "I am starting to get very nervous," a young woman wrote. "I already had a first round interview and thought it went fantastic. However I have not heard back yet about a second round interview. My classmates are already discussing the date for their second round interview. So I was wondering since I haven't heard anything yet and other students have, does that mean that I am not being offered a second round interview?"

Certainly, recruiting on social networking sites carries some risks. The Wall, for instance, attracts the occasional skeptic or critic. One visitor questioned whether companies are sincere in their claims that they don't overwork their employees. He wondered how E&Y can honestly promise work-life balance, especially during the busy tax season. Dan Black, director of Americas campus recruiting for E&Y, replied: "I can't speak for the other firms, but we do the best we can to help with work/life balance. This means different things for different people, so

E&Y does not offer a one-size-fits-all environment. Are there going to be busy times? Absolutely—plenty of them. Any company that tells you that it's all going to be fun and games and 9-to-5 is probably not giving you an accurate picture."

Then there was this tirade on the Wall: "Personally, I'm sick and tired of putting on a fake smile and constantly trying to prove myself. I've got the grades, I've got the experience, I have exactly what you need. What more do you want? Next time I'm thinking about wearing a clown costume and performing some tricks. Heck, even the interviewers gotta be sick and tired of the same personality they're always gonna see. Maybe that way I'll really stick in their mind. So I think I might give it a shot, or I'm just gonna reverse the question, 'Why do you wanna work for us?' and say 'Why do you want me to work for you?'"

E&Y seems comfortable with such comments and doesn't remove them from the Wall. It has censored a few posts that included vulgarity, but otherwise says it isn't acting like Big Brother. There was some initial resistance, however, to the Facebook site at E&Y. "It was quite a struggle to sell the Facebook idea to the company," says Black. "You give up some control because it's a free forum driven by users of the site. It isn't like a corporate Web site or brochure."

As of early 2008, E&Y had attracted more than 13,000 members to its Facebook site. The firm has hired a few people through Facebook, but considers it primarily a branding tool. "It's incumbent on us to change the image of accounting as a dull, conservative profession," Black says. "We're trying to show the Facebook generation that we're willing to speak in their language and that we're not their father's accounting firm."

The growing recruiting activity on social networking sites isn't entirely corporate. With the war in Iraq posing a major recruiting challenge, the U.S. Army is reaching out to potential enlistees on MySpace. Visitors to the Army page can chat with "Sgt. Star," their virtual guide, about joining up; listen to podcasts; view Army photos; or download an action video game about the Army Special Forces. There are also links to the MySpace pages of "the Army's friends," mostly soldiers, and a message board. Sample postings: "I hope everyone has a safe month. Take care troops. God bless" and "I have some really cool pictures of the 0.50 caliber machine gun being fired! Check them out! My company also leaves really soon to Afghanistan! Hoo-ah!"

The Army chose MySpace because of its broad reach and the ability to customize and add branding elements to its page. It planned to join Facebook as well to tap into a network of ROTC cadets. The Army's strategy is to be as ubiquitous as possible with the millennial generation. Although it still does plenty of face-to-face recruiting, the Army hopes its Web site and social networking pages will encourage young men and women to start making their decision about enlisting before they ever meet a recruiter. The Army finds that millennials like to investigate what it has to offer online with anonymity and without a recruiter breathing down their necks trying to influence them.

Clearly, the Army has its work cut out for it in trying to persuade millennials to consider a military career. Its research found that young people today have a very low propensity to sign up for military service and that the Army is viewed as "ordinary" and less elite than the Marines and Air Force. "The key is to get young people talking about the Army on their social networks and visiting our Web site," says Lt. Col. Shawn Buck, chief of the market research and analysis division of the U.S. Army Accessions Command. "We need to be in a lot of spaces to make an impression and get the Army into this generation's decision set."

CORPORATE CAREER SITES

Many companies are still focusing more on their own corporate careers Web pages than on social networking sites. That's wise, because millennials are indeed perusing them closely in their quest for the ideal job. The National Association of Colleges and Employers surveyed graduating students in 2007 and found that 81% said they frequently visited company Web sites, making it the most common job-search activity.

Jessica Foster's internship search illustrates just how significant recruiting Web sites have become in the battle for talent. The law student at Washington University in St. Louis spent hours combing law firms' Web sites. "I spent at least an hour on each firm's Web site to see their different practices and what the people and culture were like; it was one of the major factors for me in looking for a job," she says. "The Web sites also helped me gain information about the firm to use in my cover letters and interviews."

Yet she and other students find that far too many career pages lack pizzazz. They tend to be a dull assemblage of short text items describing the company and its workplace environment in vague, general terms. They are so plain vanilla that they're almost interchangeable with other companies' pedestrian careers Web sites.

So what will engage millennials? To get their attention, careers Web sites must address the generation's hot buttons: work-life balance, training and development, corporate social and environmental responsibility, and diversity. The most effective Web pages also provide a vivid sense of the corporate culture and a look at specific jobs, typically through video interviews, employee profiles, case studies, virtual tours, blogs, and podcasts.

Goldman Sachs Group Inc. realized that it needed a livelier careers site and revamped it in 2007 to give it a slicker, hipper visual design and to focus more on the investment banking firm's employees. But the firm realizes that the millennials are savvy and want much more than sizzle. Consequently, the information on Goldman's careers site is still quite substantive, including a videotaped speech by company president and co-COO Jon Winkelried at the University of Chicago, his alma matter, to a sea of students in black business suits. He talks about the firm's culture and the fact that more than half of its revenue is now generated outside the United States. The careers site also offers an interactive quiz—"Where Do I Fit In?"—to help potential applicants figure out which areas of Goldman's business might be a good match for them.

Some companies are letting employees speak their mind in blogs on their corporate and careers Web sites. But not surprisingly, many of these blogs come off as sanitized PR, with mostly raves and few, if any, rants about the company. Such one-sided blogging is more likely to alienate than appeal to millennials, who definitely resent the phoniness of trying to disguise PR spinning as unfiltered blogging.

There are some blogs, however, that do seem a bit more balanced and provide some useful insights. Take, for example, Accenture's Web site, which includes blogs from both its consultants and recruiters. In many of the postings, recently hired employees describe their assignments and challenges at the management consulting firm, generally delivering very upbeat messages. But one blogger told about the disconcerting new experience of being on "bench time" between assignments and trying not to treat it like vacation. The blogger also discussed the unnerving process of trying to secure an appropriate project and compared it to being interviewed for a job.

On Accenture's recruiting blog, there's plenty of advice for applicants, ranging from keeping cover letters professional (resist pointing out that "I'm cute and fun to be around") and behaving properly during telephone interviews (listen closely before responding, take your gum out of your mouth, and don't eat lunch while speaking).

Millennials value their experiences very highly and want a window into the company they're considering applying to. They seek a genuine feel for what it's like to work for a specific company and gravitate to sites with video profiles of younger people they can relate to. Some companies wisely let young employees chat about their personal interests, as well as the nature of their jobs, to convey that they care about work-life balance.

Germany's Deutsche Bank has created a video-oriented Web site that includes such features as a day in the life of several of its employees. One vignette showcases a soccer player who works part-time in the bank's finance division in Frankfurt, Germany. It follows her from the gym to the company coffee bar to her desk, where she works with foreign currencies. In the Let's Talk section of the site, Tim, a young analyst in equity capital markets in London, says he likes the selling process and the satisfaction of meeting short-term goals, but isn't so fond of having to "power through" loads of documents.

The most appealing careers Web sites strive to be entertaining as well as informative. As unlikely as it might sound, law firm sites are among the most inventive and playful. To overcome the starchy, button-down image and the specter of long hours of monotonous work, some firms are delivering a hip, humorous message in the recruiting battle for the most coveted law school prospects.

The Morrison & Foerster law firm takes a very witty approach with its careers site, which certainly ranks as one of the most inspired on the Internet. For example, it features a section titled Pigeonholed that shows plenty of pictures of pigeons and asks, "Did you go to law school dreaming of drafting high yield covenants? Or maybe doing document production? Somehow those scenes never made it into *Law & Order* or *Ally McBeal*. Hmm, must have ended up on the cutting room floor." The firm goes on to say, "Will you be just one more unit of lawyer taking up residence in a new roost? Cushy roost for two to three years. Mind-numbing work. . . . Here we raise amazing lawyers; we leave the cultivation of pigeons to others."

In the Achievements section of the site, Morrison & Foerster doesn't simply tout its place in various law firm rankings; it lets you create your own rankings of the ugliest vegetables (choices include horseradish, artichoke, truffle), strangest celebrity names (Apple, Satchel, Nell Marmalade), and the most addictive snack foods (french fries, Oreos, Doritos).

Another law firm—Choate, Hall & Stewart—overhauled its careers site in 2007 to try to stand out from the crowd with millennial generation law students. "There is intense competition for top-tier law students, and we needed to increase our appeal to this generation with a more striking Web site," explains John Ventola, cochairman of Choate's hiring committee and summer program. "The new site has created a lot of buzz at law schools. Many students found it amusing and informative; some didn't like it, but at least it made an impression and showed that we have a different mentality than other firms." Choate saw a "dramatic increase" in interest in the firm during the fall 2007 recruiting season, he adds, and more students accepted invitations for second-round interviews than in previous years.

To differentiate the firm from bigger competitors, some of the Web site's videos pit Choate against Megafirm, in a style very similar to Apple Inc.'s Mac versus PC commercials. In one spot, the actor playing Megafirm is frazzled because he can't find his lost briefcase and can't keep track of all of his firm's offices; in another, Megafirm wears his suit and brings his briefcase to the beach. The actress playing Choate, meanwhile, is focused on clients, not office locations, and is free to relax on vacation. But that last message didn't ring true with everyone. One cynical visitor to the site posted this comment: "Since when did associates get vacations?"

The firm's summer interns star in other videos. Their comments don't really have anything to do with work. But that's the point. The takeaway message is that there's more to life than a job if you work for Choate. Amelia Stewart, a student at Boston College, says she wrote a thesis on horror films and that *The Shining* is her favorite; Michael Oliviero, a student at Emory University, tells about joining a Swedish folk group whose songs are like a blend of Mister Rogers and John Denver. "But don't worry," he says. "I'm not going to sing for you."

Jessica Foster, the dedicated Web site searcher at Washington University, also appears on Choate's Web site, having ended up at the firm for her internship in 2007. Choate's old site helped attract her to the firm, but she finds the new version much more fun and enticing. In her video clip, she chats about her love of downhill skiing and her pride in running in her first marathon. "The videos provide a look at the personalities at the firm," she says, "and that is one of the major factors for my generation in looking for a job."

MOVIES AND GAMES

To score points with millennials, some recruiters are playing to the generation's video and gaming culture. KPMG challenged its interns to create videos about integrity and picked a spoof of the television series *The Office* as winner. Similarly, Boston Consulting Group Inc., a management consulting firm, invited students to create two-minute videos about what strategy is and why it's important. "We allowed millennials to show their stuff," says Kermit King, senior partner and head of recruiting for the Americas. "We were looking for originality and saliency. In classic millennial fashion, the videos were all about them."

Boston Consulting's winning video: "The Coffee Interns." Two interns race to be first to fetch coffee for one of the firm's consultants, seeing "a window of opportunity for a promotion." Their strategies range from "asset management—utilizing physical resources" by driving to a coffee shop to "networking—engaging human capital" by phoning in the coffee order so that it's ready and waiting. Ultimately, both lose to a third intern who applied the "fixing the root of the problem—thinking beyond the cup" strategy and quickly brewed a pot of coffee at the office.

Some recruiters include video games on career pages and social networking sites, along with computer screen savers and wallpaper. GoArmy.com, for example, is highly interactive in trying to bring the military experience alive on young people's computers. The site offers camouflage design and other wallpaper patterns and such video games as Army Target Practice, Basic Rifle Marksmanship, Patriot Missile System Simulation, and Blackhawk Challenge. The Army Active Desktop lets users switch to night vision, add patches and medals, and rotate and flip vehicles. Potential recruits also can listen to such tunes as "The Army Goes Rolling Along" and soldiers' marching music.

Other recruiters, such as L'Oréal, Procter & Gamble Co., and Groupe Danone, encourage students to play strategy games that promote the company and help the employers spot promising talent. Some contests are open to undergraduate and graduate students; others are limited to M.B.A.s. Through the business simulation games, companies can see students in action, demonstrating creativity, tactical thinking, teamwork, and persuasion skills.

The games, which are typically played at least partly online, change from year to year. Procter & Gamble's Just in Case competition, for instance, has focused on its Olay and Swiffer brands and challenged players to identify the next company P&G should acquire. With more emphasis on corporate responsibility today, the French food and beverage company Groupe Danone created an international management game called Trust. It requires students to formulate a profitable three-year business strategy for a Groupe Danone subsidiary, while taking into consideration social, environmental, and ethical issues and retaining "the trust of all the company's stakeholders."

"Students see these games as more fun and engaging than the usual company information sessions and receptions," says Steve Pollock, cofounder of WetFeet Inc., a recruiting consulting firm. In addition, the games enable companies to reach out to many more campuses than recruiters could ever visit. For example, L'Oréal's e-Strat Challenge marketing game attracted about 44,000 students from 128 countries in 2007.

L'Oréal particularly hoped the game would change its image with male students. It was perceived as a little old-fashioned and as a company more for women, but now it believes that e-Strat has helped it demonstrate that L'Oréal is a modern, world-class employer. In e-Strat, student teams run a virtual cosmetics company called Prima, whose cyber-competitors include Diva, Bella, Vista, and Mirror.com. They must make dozens of decisions as they manage new brands, Web sites, distribution channels, advertising budgets, and research and development. Should they sell in discount or department stores? Is their target market families or singles, the affluent or low income? Aware of the millennial generation's interest in corporate citizenship, L'Oréal has added diversity and social and environmental responsibility issues to the game.

Each team's online performance is measured with an index that reflects market share, profitability, research and development quality, and customer satisfaction. In the end, finalists travel to L'Oréal's Paris headquarters to defend their business plans before a panel of judges. In addition to a possible job offer, winners receive a trip to the destination of their choice.

L'Oréal clearly has become the grand master of strategy games. In addition to e-Strat for both M.B.A. and undergraduate students, there's Brandstorm, in which undergraduates act as marketing managers for such brands as Lancôme and Garnier, and Ingenius, in which engineering and supply chain students take on an industrial project. "The games give us a direct link to the Internet generation," says François de Wazières, L'Oréal's director of international recruitment. "They're a smart way to show what it's like inside L'Oréal and to let students see the company's global scope and opportunities for a fast-paced career."

CASTING A WIDER NET

As demand for millennial graduates increases in the next few years, companies must extend their reach to more candidates without necessarily visiting more campuses. That means figuring out creative virtual recruiting ploys like L'Oréal's games.

Some companies are expanding their talent searches by trolling through blogs and message boards on job-oriented and other Web sites for prime candidates. They might, for instance, read a posting about a negative experience that an intern or ex-employee had while working for a competitor and reach out to the disgruntled prospect with an e-mail or text message.

FedEx Corp. recruiters read blogs where young people often express their personal passions. They're looking for a match between the individual's and the firm's interests and values. "Our recruiting slogan is 'connecting people to their passions,'" says John Leech, FedEx's director of recruitment. For example, if a blogger shows a strong environmental commitment, a recruiter might send a message pointing out that FedEx is investing in "green" vehicles. The company might also contact fans of the movie *Cast Away*, in which actor Tom Hanks played a FedEx manager who ends up on a deserted island after a plane crash and manages to deliver one of the surviving packages after he returns to civilization. The reasoning: if they liked the movie and its heroic portrayal of a FedEx employee, they might consider a career opportunity at the company.

"We call this passive recruiting," says Leech. "It leads to an introduction with people who aren't necessarily posting their resumes online." The World Wide Web certainly offers a vast hunting ground for talent. But the impatient, multitasking millennials are elusive prey. They're curious, flitting from site to site and always discovering new blogs and social networks. That's why Leech's recruiting team includes a "candidate intelligence adviser," who studies how the millennial generation works, lives, and communicates. "We need to be as creative and innovative as this new generation, if not more so," Leech says.

FedEx also tried an online career fair for information technology jobs that allowed people to send text messages directly to hiring managers. "The job candidates loved it; the hiring managers hated it," Leech says. "The managers didn't like shorthand messages like TTYL (translation: talk to you later), and they didn't like not hearing the other person's voice, because they couldn't tell if they could communicate well." For future online career fairs, the company plans to spend more time preparing managers and selecting ones who are more savvy about texting.

"Baby-boomer generation recruiters still love to set up a booth with our purple tablecloths, hand out free pens, and shake hands," Leech says. "But that isn't what millennials want. They like to hear from us online. And if they're concerned about the environment, they appreciate that we're not using all that airline fuel to fly to their campus."

Online resume banks provide another way to cast a wider net and connect more effectively with millennials. That has been part of Whirlpool Corp.'s digital recruiting strategy. The appliance maker continues to do on-campus recruiting at its "executive campuses"—Harvard University, Indiana University, University of Notre Dame, University of Illinois, Michigan State University, Ohio State University, Purdue University, University of Michigan, and University of Chicago. But the company also seeks talent from a large group of other schools, such as Duke University, Dartmouth College, Northwestern University, University of California at Los Angeles and Berkeley, University of Texas, University of Southern California, University of North Carolina, and Clark Atlanta University, through campus recruiting events and by reviewing resumes online. The company conducts telephone screenings of the most promising students it finds in an online resume database, and if it likes what it hears, it brings them into its global headquarters for further assessment.

Whirlpool also has been testing a technology that allows students to answer a set of questions via a remote PC-based video camera. That approach extends the company's reach to more students without even requiring a recruiter to do the phone screen. The recorded interviews are stored on a secure Web site that only a Whirlpool recruiter can access.

"I believe recruiting will become more and more virtual," says Tiffany Voglewede, a university recruiter and program manager at Whirlpool. "We cannot afford to recruit only from our executive campuses because other schools, including some smaller schools, have amazing students."

Greg Ruf, CEO of MBA Focus, which promotes its online resume database to companies for virtual recruiting, believes that employers must change their way of thinking to reach the millennials. "To be successful in the future, recruiters will need a different skill set," he says. "Rather than being event planners who are transaction oriented, they'll need to become more adept and comfortable with technology and the online world."

He tries to persuade companies to search resumes online for top prospects and then reach out to them with a personalized electronic message that might include a link to the corporate careers Web site. "Millennial generation students want to be contacted virtually," he says. "The students and their schools are totally stressed out by all the recruiters who are spending so much time on campus."

But it's important that online recruiting be personal and engaging. Given the deluge of information they receive daily, students will likely consider it spam if a recruiter's e-mail is nothing more than a generic corporate pitch. They want personalized messages and prefer communicating through instant messaging and texting rather than e-mail because they want immediate feedback.

Whirlpool, for example, introduced a new marketing tool to send text messages to students to inform them of recruiting events, resume submission deadlines, and interview opportunities. The company also is launching a live chat feature on its online careers site, assigning employees from different departments to answer questions at designated times. "Today's college graduates want someone right there when they have a question," says Voglewede. "Many college students have expressed their preference to communicate interactively with someone rather than just read someone's observations about the company in a blog, so we're pursuing the chat route."

THE PERSONAL TOUCH

The days of wining and dining students aren't over yet. Virtual recruiting clearly has its limitations and must be supplemented with personal interaction as a company narrows its list of prime candidates. Face-to-face meetings in social settings and interview rooms allow both the company and job applicant to size each other up and decide whether they're a good fit. After all, recruiting really is all about matchmaking skills. An active recruiting company spends hundreds of thousands of dollars a year to try to bring the best and brightest millennials on board. It can't afford to make many bad matches.

Deloitte & Touche's recruiters and executives are limiting their virtual recruiting and spending additional time at their more than 40 target schools, getting to know students better. "There's a fine balance between how much you use technology and how much you do in person; students still want to hear and talk to people directly," says Diane Borhani, U.S. national campus recruiting leader at Deloitte, an accounting and consulting firm. "I've also learned that students prefer that we interact with them through our own careers site and through other professional careers sites more so than through personal social networking sites, such as MySpace."

Karen Calo of IBM agrees. "I'm not sure Second Life and other new technologies will ever totally replace traditional recruiting," she says. "You can only see students' intellectual curiosity, excitement, and body language in a face-to-face situation." Even as it goes more high-tech in its recruiting, IBM also is trying to increase personal contact. It is organizing "power panels" at some schools, for example, bringing IBM executives, local companies, government officials, and business partners together to discuss job skills and opportunities.

To try to make a stronger impression, some companies hope to form tighter relationships with prime prospects through more intimate events, such as dinners with only 10 students rather than a mass cocktail party. They are assigning "buddy employees" to hot prospects to help woo them, and they are making a more concerted push to close the deal once a job offer has been extended. Opera Solutions, a boutique consulting firm, assigns each of its M.B.A. picks to a "cultivation team," a group of employees who offer the student advice and information about Opera and its projects and arrange visits to the company's office. The firm wanted to ensure that students who are offered positions become very familiar with its culture to increase acceptance rates. Opera believes that this approach helped it recruit students who had offers from other top consulting companies and that it could lead to higher retention rates.

Wachovia Corp. believes strongly in the power of personal networking, too, and it has created some clever and distinctive social events to appeal to millennials. At some schools, Wachovia recruiters and senior managers interact with students at wine tastings and cooking classes. Giving its own spin to speed dating, the company also invites students to speed-networking events where they talk with Wachovia representatives for 15 minutes until a bell rings and then move to the next table. The meetings may be brief, but at least students can connect with everyone.

Especially popular are the financial services company's poker tournaments where M.B.A. students play cards and socialize with senior leaders from Wachovia and their business school's alumni who work at the company. Wachovia chose poker because the gambling game has become so popular with young people. The company feared it might attract only men, but women showed up as well.

"This generation loves to network, but not at a formal dinner where they're stuck talking to the same person all evening," says Kanika Raney, Wachovia's campus recruiting chief. "With our recruiting events, we try to show that we're not as stuffy as some of our competitors in investment banking."

TARGETING PRE-COLLEGE TEENS

Although companies are most concerned about attracting college, law, M.B.A., and other graduate school students to fill their talent pipelines, a few farsighted recruiters are even reaching out to younger millennials in middle schools and high schools. That's because achievement-oriented millennials are making career plans earlier than ever. Research studies commissioned by Deloitte & Touche revealed that nearly half of 12- to 14-year-old students have started to think seriously about careers. By the time they're 17 or 18, many are locked into a career path. But business careers are seldom on the young millennials' radar screens. To Deloitte's dismay, only 2.3% of 12- to 18-year-olds surveyed showed interest in accounting or consulting. Many teens, the firm found, have reservations about working for big business because they perceive it to be too focused on profits and not enough on people.

Those findings prompted Deloitte to launch a pre-college outreach program that includes a career guidebook and Web site and an online business simulation competition peppered with games and music. In the online business game, high school teams of four students stage a festival that raises virtual money for the United Way's Operation Graduation campaign to encourage people to stay in school. The goal is to teach about business, ethics, money, and decision making, as well as the importance of volunteer activities for charitable organizations. In the end, Deloitte makes donations to the winning schools' local United Way chapters.

The career guidebook includes a few profiles of Deloitte employees, along with people in other occupations, plus a "commercial message" from W. Stanton Smith, national director of Next Generation Initiatives at Deloitte & Touche. He asks teenagers to consider a career they may never have imagined: professional auditor. "Boring, you say? Are you sure?" Smith asks. "A lot of careers that don't have television shows or action movies built around them still have plenty to hold your interest (and there is a professional auditor who plays a key role in at least one classic action movie, *The Untouchables*). . . . This is a profession which makes a difference. Auditors keep the system honest by making sure that individuals and corporations and governments are responsible for the money that passes through their hands."

Deloitte may make some progress in elevating the reputation of the accounting industry. But it will be a hard sell to the millennial generation, which certainly remembers the demise of Enron Corp. and its auditor Arthur Andersen over accounting fraud just a few short years ago.

CHAPTER HIGHLIGHTS

- Recruiters are connecting with millennials on their own turf by creating company pages on Facebook and other popular social networking sites. But the strategy could backfire if companies become too intrusive.

- Corporate career Web sites should address millennial generation hot buttons: work-life balance, training and development, social and environmental responsibility, and diversity.

- Playing to the generation's video and gaming culture, companies are inviting students to play strategy games on their Web sites and are offering jobs to some of the most talented competitors.

- To cast a wider net, recruiters are searching for candidates on blogs, in chat rooms, and through online resume databases.

- The personal touch is still important. But to impress jaded millennials, companies must be more creative in their on-campus recruiting and try such new tactics as poker tournaments and wine tastings.

- It's never too early to start the recruiting process. Companies should consider reaching out to millennials in the middle school and high school years when they are beginning to choose careers.

10

Dream Jobs

What would be the ultimate dream job for the millennial generation?

Well, it would definitely have to provide unlimited career opportunities, plenty of praise and rewards, flexible work hours, a casual and fun atmosphere, and, of course, a meteoric rise to the executive suite. But when it comes to specific companies and industries, the millennials are much less of one mind about the perfect job.

Management consulting and accounting firms, innovative technology companies, nonprofit organizations, and government agencies certainly rate high on this generation's wish list. Some millennials seek the stability of established and reputable companies like General Electric Co. and Procter & Gamble Co., while others favor small and medium-size businesses where they believe they will enjoy greater access to senior executives and take on major responsibilities from the get-go. Alternatively, a growing number of young people are bypassing the corporate world entirely and striking out on their own to satisfy entrepreneurial passions.

Of course, after a few months on the job, millennials may not be so starry-eyed. This exploratory generation is likely to bounce from one seemingly dreamy job to another before finally settling on a long-term career. But at least while they're still students, they believe they know which jobs will be just right for them.

Teenagers are thinking mainly in terms of careers rather than specific employers. Business careers are most popular with male teenagers, whereas female teens most want to become doctors and teachers, according to a survey by Junior Achievement, an organization that helps prepare young people for the workplace (see accompanying table). More than half of the survey respondents said they are motivated mainly by their passion for a particular vocation, and only 12% said money influences their career choices.

Teenagers' Top Career Choices

Career	Percentage of Males Selecting This Career	Percentage of Females Selecting This Career
Business	14.0	7.5
Doctor	3.8	10.0
Teacher	3.0	9.6
Professional athlete	9.4	1.4
Computer industry	7.8	1.9
Entertainer	4.9	3.7
Lawyer	2.2	4.2
Veterinarian	0.6	5.2
Engineer	5.3	1.3

Source: Junior Achievement, 2007

At the college and graduate school level, millennials are more experienced and have very definite notions of their ideal employers. They clearly favor companies with cool images, most notably technology pioneers Google Inc. and Apple Inc., both of which received very high scores in student surveys conducted by the research firm Universum in 2008 (see accompanying tables).

Students see Google, which placed first in the rankings, as a fast-growing, visionary company. They also like its unconventional office environment and youthful, multicultural workforce. From gourmet cafeterias and hair styling salons to massage therapy and video games, Google piles on the perks and lets employees blend their work and personal lives at its Googleplex headquarters in Mountain View, California. Among

Ideal Employers for Undergraduate College Students

Rank	Employer
1	Google
2	Walt Disney
3	Apple
4	Ernst & Young
5	U.S. State Department
6	Goldman Sachs
7	Deloitte
8	Peace Corps
9	National Aeronautics and Space Administration
10	PricewaterhouseCoopers
11	Teach for America
12	Central Intelligence Agency
13	Microsoft
14	Federal Bureau of Investigation
15	J.P. Morgan Chase
16	KPMG
17	Nike
18	Johnson & Johnson
19	Merrill Lynch
20	Mayo Clinic

Source: Universum, 2008

the top 10 reasons Google gives for joining the company: "Work and play are not mutually exclusive. It is possible to code and pass the puck at the same time."

Google also has a philosophy of valuing ability over experience—a definite plus with millennials, who much prefer a meritocracy to a seniority-based workplace. Young people also warm to Google's inclusive, nonhierarchical culture. "We know that every employee has something important to say and that every employee is integral to our success," the company states on its jobs Web page. "And where else can a newbie unabashedly and unflinchingly skate over a corporate officer during a roller hockey game?"

Universum has detected growing undergraduate interest in nonprofit organizations and government agencies, including the U.S. State Department, National Aeronautics and Space Administration, Central Intelligence Agency, Peace Corps, and Teach for America. Such employers may prove to be a good match for the millennials because of their desire to perform meaningful work and make a contribution to society. Undergraduates also aspire to work at the major accounting firms, banks, and consumer goods companies.

M.B.A. students, in contrast, are aiming more for high-paying jobs and favor a different mix of employers. Consulting and investment banking firms perennially dominate the top spots in Universum's M.B.A. rankings. "The firms whose people are its product—investment banking, consulting, and professional services—are doing the most outstanding job in attracting this generation of M.B.A.s," says Claudia Tattanelli, CEO of Universum USA. "But M.B.A. students today also have become more interested in some of the big consumer-brand companies like Nike and Walt Disney."

Many millennials hope to work for companies they respect and consider to be solid corporate citizens, such as Target Corp. and Starbucks Corp. This idealistic generation witnessed the wave of corporate scandals that began with the collapse of Enron Corp. in 2001, and want to steer clear of any employer with a checkered past. The public relations firm Hill & Knowlton surveyed M.B.A. students at 12 international business schools in 2007 and found that about three-quarters believe that corporate reputation is highly important in choosing an employer. An additional 20% consider reputation fairly important. In rating specific industries, the M.B.A.s gave negative reputation scores to oil, pharmaceutical, chemical, alcoholic

Ideal Employers for M.B.A. Students

Rank	Employer
1	Google
2	McKinsey
3	Goldman Sachs
4	Apple
5	Boston Consulting Group
6	Bain
7	Walt Disney
8	Nike
9	Deloitte
10	J.P. Morgan Chase
11	General Electric
12	Microsoft
13	Johnson & Johnson
14	Procter & Gamble
15	Morgan Stanley
16	Lehman Brothers
17	Starbucks
18	Merrill Lynch
19	Coca-Cola
20	BMW

Source: Universum, 2008

beverage, and tobacco companies and said they would have little interest in working for them.

Some millennials prefer large employers like GE and Johnson & Johnson because they promise a wealth of job opportunities at their many business units around the globe. Millennials also find the financial strength and stability of such corporate titans reassuring. "When this generation grew up, the world order was crumbling around them, with terrorism, Enron, and the Catholic Church scandals," says Kaye Foster-Cheek, vice president for human resources at Johnson & Johnson. "So young people are looking for stable companies that have stood the test of time in terms of their values and financial performance. Millennials find Johnson & Johnson's Credo statement of values, which has been guiding us for about 65 years, very appealing, but at the same time, they want to be sure that the Credo doesn't make us stodgy."

Some young people are intrigued by jobs that give them freedom to try out different roles. For example, two-year rotational programs are popular with business school graduates because they get a chance to do stints in different departments without locking themselves into a particular role.

Matthew Cromwell didn't start out in a rotational program, but he did take a job that allows him to explore his options for a little while longer. As manager of corporate administration for Excellus Blue Cross Blue Shield in Rochester, New York, his job changes from day to day. "I'm not confined to finance or marketing or any other function, so work never feels dull," says the M.B.A. graduate from the University of Rochester. "I work frequently with a number of different senior managers and get the chance to investigate a lot of areas of the company to see what I'm most attracted to."

Before he joined Excellus, for example, he didn't realize that he enjoyed making presentations and doing other communications-related assignments. "I always thought I would end up in something more mathematical like finance or accounting," he says, "but I find that I really like learning different ways to communicate a point to a specific audience."

CONSULTING TRADE-OFFS

Management consulting's popularity with millennials is somewhat surprising, but it serves to illustrate the conflicting priorities of this generation. Despite their desire for flexible schedules and a balance between work and play, many young people are willing to travel and put in long hours to land a lucrative and engaging consulting job.

Indeed, consulting seems to satisfy the two most important factors M.B.A. students consider when choosing a job. In an Aspen Institute survey of M.B.A.s at 15 business schools in 2007, respondents were asked to name the three top factors in their job search. "Challenging and diverse responsibilities" ranked first, mentioned by about two-thirds of respondents, followed by "compensation," named by about half of the students. Close behind in third place: "work-life balance" (about 45% of respondents).

Some millennials are drawn to consulting because they want to avoid the dreaded sameness syndrome of many corporate jobs. "I hate being bored, and I know that if I get bored, I will slack off," says Paige Marino, who joined a consulting firm after receiving her M.B.A. degree from the University of California at Davis. "Variety is very important to me. If I had to sit in a cube by myself and do the same thing every day, I would want to die."

The team-oriented nature of consulting also appeals to Marino, who became quite accustomed to group projects in business school. "I am able to work through problems better when I can bounce ideas off others," she explains. "Also, teamwork breeds a certain kind of healthy conflict that makes the outcome better. It is good for people to challenge what I think and for me to challenge them."

Nicholas Riolo, an M.B.A. student at the Tuck School of Business at Dartmouth College, readily acknowledges that management consulting hardly allows for "a smooth, laid-back lifestyle." He should know, having worked as a health insurance industry consultant at Accenture before starting business school. Nevertheless, he plans to return to consulting after graduation because he has found that the learning and stimulation more than compensate for the demanding hours.

"If you find yourself in a project that you don't like, you know it will be over in two months," he says. "I'm happy to pay my dues if I'm learning a lot and have an ever changing mix of work assignments, teammates, and bosses. In consulting, I never feel that I'm just rubber-stamping and pushing papers."

Some millennials also like consulting because many firms encourage employees to perform volunteer work. Riolo, for example, volunteered as a consultant and mentor to developing businesses in Los Angeles. He worked with a formerly homeless woman who was selling her jewelry at the beach and trying to move into retail stores. "It was a kind of turning point for me," he says, "because it showed me that business is a great way to help make people's dreams come true."

As for the work-life balance issue, Riolo has been talking with Dartmouth alumni who work in consulting about how they manage to raise a family and pursue other interests, especially given the heavy travel schedule. "I haven't come to terms yet with how I'm going to handle it," he says. "Because of the project-based work, a lot of consulting companies are able to offer sabbaticals, part-time programs, healthy vacation time, or partial work-from-home situations. That being said, I still know that I will have to make certain personal sacrifices to continue along the career path I have chosen."

From their perspective, consulting firms believe they are attracting millennials because they provide a good springboard to other careers. "For millennials, consulting's appeal is deeper than just that it's interesting work," says Kermit King, senior partner and head of recruiting for the Americas at Boston Consulting Group Inc. "They don't know that they'll be consultants for life; they may start a business in two years or aspire to be a CEO. The note we need to sound to keep attracting this generation is that if you come here for five years and then go into industry, you can be sure that the road through BCG will have made you a better leader."

VENTURING OUT ON THEIR OWN

Reagan Pollack didn't feel that he needed the leadership grooming of a consulting position, or any other corporate job for that matter. Before he even started filling out college application forms, he knew he was destined to pursue a career "off the corporate beaten track." After all, entrepreneurship was considered "a family gene" dating back to his great-grandfather, and his father had always advised him, "Do what you love, and the money will follow."

But what exactly would he love to do? An acoustic and electric guitar player, Pollack considered a musical career but decided he would probably end up being just another failed artist. There was also his family's party balloon business to consider, but he really wanted a passion of his own. So he enrolled at Babson College in Wellesley, Massachusetts, a hotbed of programs for budding entrepreneurs, and before long he had his "aha" moment. He believed he could give a boost to the careers of musical performers by launching an online service called WorldMusicLink that connects music industry professionals and artists.

"For my parent's generation, corporations had a certain standing, and it was an achievement to get a job with them," Pollack says. "But we millennials aren't focused on one company and its values. We want to create new value through our new ventures. My vision is a marketplace that bridges the fragmented pieces of the music industry so professionals can connect with each other and prosper. One of my goals is to eliminate the struggling musical artist."

Pollack and many other millennials are rejecting corporate life to follow their dreams. Entrepreneurship may in fact prove to be the perfect career path for the millennials who don't want to end up as "corporate slaves" and are willing to take risks to marry their talents with their passions. By starting their own businesses, they can immediately do something personally meaningful rather than wait for a company to give them that chance. They say they want to succeed or fail based on the merits of their endeavors, not the whims of a corporate boss.

To be sure, entrepreneurs must put in long hours and sacrifice much of their personal life. But they can try to blend their personal and professional lives, especially if they run their businesses from their homes.

"I have some friends at big public companies," Pollack says, "and I give them one to two years at most. The reputations of the companies bring them in the door, but they soon feel disconnected and like they're just a spoke in the wheel."

Because of students like Pollack, many business schools have expanded their menu of entrepreneurship courses. The Wharton School at the University of Pennsylvania has added eight entrepreneurship classes to its curriculum in recent years, and 40% of its M.B.A. students now take an introductory entrepreneurship course, up from 27% in 2001.

"Students find entrepreneurship empowering," says James Wheeler, executive director of the Center for Entrepreneurial Studies at the University of Oklahoma. "They understand and embrace the sacrifices because they want to take the road less traveled. They want to impact their town, state, country, and world in a positive way, and the best way to do that is entrepreneurship." The number of undergraduate and graduate majors in entrepreneurship at Oklahoma has surged 150% over the past three years, and the number of courses has tripled.

Entrepreneurship enrollments should continue to swell. When the Ewing Marion Kauffman Foundation surveyed 8- to 21-year-olds, about 40% said they would like to start their own business, and another 37% were unsure but left open the possibility of becoming entrepreneurs. "It is gratifying to see that American youth aspire to not just take a job, but to make a job," says Dennis Cheek, vice president of education at the foundation.

Even the U.S. Army has recognized the entrepreneurship trend. To attract millennials, it is testing a program that offers as much as $40,000 in seed money for a start-up after new recruits have completed their military service. More than half of the young adults the Army surveyed said they would like to own their own businesses, but 79% expected lack of capital to be a major impediment.

Some millennials find that parents will provide a financial safety net to help them get their businesses off the ground. And if the start-up fails, millennials know they're welcome back home. Pollack, for example, has been fortunate to receive steady support from his family. His mother and sister serve on World-MusicLink's board of directors, and Pollack splits his time between his parents' home in Pebble Beach, California, and his girlfriend's place in Carmel.

Because so many resources are available through college entrepreneurship programs, consultants, mentors, and government small-business programs, Pollack believes that millennials are finding it easier than ever to start their own ventures. "This has to be one of the smoothest times in history to take a risk and create your own company," he says. "There's so much advice and information out there to demystify the art of the start-up."

The Internet and other technological advances also are helping some entrepreneurs get established. Jonathan Soares, founder of Q Products Inc., has used social networking sites and mass e-mailings to help whet consumers' appetite for his gourmet barbecue sauces. The entrepreneurial bug bit Soares early in life when he started his first business selling candy in middle school. He knew he wanted to be in charge and steer clear of the bureaucracy, cutthroat atmosphere, and unethical behavior he saw at too many corporations. So while attending Western Connecticut State University, he launched his line of honey, spicy Cajun, and hickory teriyaki sauces.

"Technology has created so many opportunities to start a successful business and think outside the box," Soares says. "The Internet lets me create buzz when my sauces go into a new market or when I have promotional events at bars, clubs, and supermarkets. It's great for word-of-mouth marketing." His MySpace page also has proven effective in his "personal branding strategy" of developing his "Jonny Q persona." By adding new "friends" on the social networking site, he says, "I hope to create an emotional connection with people and establish a personal brand for my barbecue sauces like Dave Thomas did with Wendy's and Orville Redenbacher did with popcorn."

Some millennials plan to work initially for a major company before going it alone. Will Wright, who is studying for both an M.B.A. and a master's degree in public health at the University of California at Berkeley, envisions eventually starting his own insurance company to help provide coverage to the millions of uninsured Americans. "It doesn't work for me to give back to the community simply by painting a house or picking up garbage," he says. "But this insurance company could be something big that would reduce the amount the country spends on health care, differentiate doctors and hospitals based on their quality, and help individual members become healthier."

First, however, he is prepared to work in the health care practice of a big consulting firm or even for an established insurance company. "I'm realizing very quickly that starting an insurance company will be both difficult and risky," says Wright, who graduated from Harvard with a degree in biology. "I want to work first in high-level health care strategy to build my knowledge and credibility in the field. If I can establish my insurance company in about 10 years when I'm in my mid-30s, I'll be very pleased."

CHAPTER HIGHLIGHTS

- Dream jobs for the millennial generation vary by age and college degree program. For teenage boys, business careers are the top choice, whereas teenage girls aspire most to be doctors and teachers. At the undergraduate level, government agencies and nonprofit organizations are quite popular, along with major accounting firms, banks, and consumer goods companies. M.B.A. students pick a mix of technology, consulting, and investment banking companies as their ideal employers.

- Corporate reputation figures heavily into the millennial generation's employment choices. They gravitate to companies they consider to be model corporate citizens, such as Starbucks and Target, and tend to avoid industries that suffer from a negative image, including oil, pharmaceuticals, chemicals, alcoholic beverages, and tobacco.

- Although hot young companies like Google are alluring, some millennials are drawn instead to large, established employers, such as General Electric and Johnson & Johnson, which offer both stability and an array of job opportunities.

- The strong interest in management consulting firms highlights the conflicting priorities of the millennial generation. Young college graduates and M.B.A. students find the diversity of projects stimulating and the generous compensation enticing, but they must sacrifice work-life balance when assignments demand long hours and frequent travel.

- More millennials are forgoing corporate careers and gambling that they can succeed as entrepreneurs. Despite the financial risks, millennials want to start their own companies to fulfill their dreams and control their own lives and careers. The Internet and other technological tools help young entrepreneurs establish their new ventures, and parents often provide a financial safety net.

11

A Generous Generation

Mira Inbar, an M.B.A. student at the University of California at Berkeley, traces her first stirrings of altruism to her childhood in southern Florida. In fact, she proudly declares that she has been "a committed environmentalist since I was three years old." She remembers feeling appalled by the rapid encroachment of commercial development on the natural habitat in her community. "When I was little, there were orange groves, wooded areas, herons, and cranes everywhere," she says wistfully. "Then I saw everything I called home disappear and turn into strip malls."

Inbar remained true to her values and went on to receive a bachelor's degree in biology and environmental studies from Oberlin College. She envisioned herself becoming a conservation biologist, but after a research stint in Costa Rica studying butterfly decline around coffee plantations, she suddenly yearned for something with greater impact. She moved on to work for nonprofit groups in Peru and Washington, DC, but finally headed for business school because she says she realized that companies hold the key to major environmental gains. "I knew a lot about insects, but not much about finance and accounting before Berkeley," she says. "After I get my M.B.A., I'd like to work in a company that's trying to change business as usual by integrating environmental criteria into everything it does."

While still at Berkeley, she is active in a student social responsibility club and is leading an initiative to cut energy consumption and make the university's Haas School of Business "carbon neutral." In explaining her generation's commitment to the environment, Inbar says she believes that young people are searching for meaning and connections beyond themselves. "We grew up in a culture of greed inundated with messages about being as rich as possible," Inbar says. "But some of us are scared about where the world is headed. If I want to have children, I had better devote myself to the environment."

Some critics accuse the millennial generation of pursuing shallow, self-centered dreams of fame and fortune. But there is really much more depth to this generation, as exemplified by millennials like Inbar. No doubt millennials seek personal success and recognition, but many of them also believe they have a higher calling. Indeed, more than 60% of 13- to 25-year-olds said they feel personally responsible for making a difference in the world, according to a 2006 survey by the communications and marketing agencies Cone Inc. and Amp Insights.

These days, millennials are certainly busy trying to live up to that responsibility. They are promoting clean energy policies at their high schools and colleges to help combat global warming. They are raising relief funds and public awareness of the crisis in Darfur. They are forgoing a boozy spring break at the beach to feed the homeless, rescue sea turtles, and work at shelters for victims of domestic abuse. After college graduation, some millennials are even putting their careers on hold and teaching in poor neighborhoods.

Millennial M.B.A. students like Inbar are bringing a new sensibility to business schools, the traditional training ground for investment bankers and management consultants. "Today's M.B.A.s are looking for unconventional ways to use their leadership skills in society and do much more than make money," says Paul Danos, dean of the Tuck School of Business at Dartmouth College. "It's very likely that their path to success will include a blending of corporate and public activities. Ethics, sustainability, poverty, health, and global economic development are just as important to them as balance sheets and marketing studies." But, he adds, millennials may have to struggle "to resist the tempting lucrative opportunities for top M.B.A. graduates if they want to contribute to society in a major way."

Why do millennials feel such a strong philanthropic instinct? America's education system clearly deserves some of the credit. Many millennials were encouraged or even required to perform good deeds to graduate from middle school and high school. Giving back has become second nature to them. At the same time, television and the Internet brought millennials closer to such calamities as Hurricane Katrina and the bloody strife in Darfur. The impact of the terrorist attacks of September 11, 2001, may also be a factor. Millennials were shaken by that traumatic day and witnessed the heroism of rescue workers and volunteers at Ground Zero in New York City.

"One bright spot coming out of the 9/11 tragedy is a surge of interest by college students in serving their community," says Steve Goldsmith, chairman of the federal Corporation for National and Community Service. According to a report by his organization, 3.3 million college students volunteered in 2005, nearly 600,000 more than in 2002. Similarly, the Higher Education Research Institute at the University of California at Los Angeles found that two-thirds of college freshmen in 2006 considered helping others to be an important value, the highest level in 20 years.

"What resonates most with the college students I meet is the possibility of making a difference," says Matt Kramer, president of Teach for America, which places college graduates in teaching positions in low-income communities. "We entered a phase after September 11, where more young people looked up to people like Bill Clinton, Laura Bush, Bill Gates, and Barack Obama. They became the rock stars of society." Indeed, many millennials were drawn to presidential candidate Obama because his message of change matched their idealistic vision of a better world. Some millennials even took to calling themselves Generation Obama.

Although some millennials crave wealth, many say they quickly find that money alone isn't rewarding enough. "I was essentially helping rich people get even richer," says Tracy Cheung, describing how she began feeling after working a few years as an analyst in Lehman Brothers Inc.'s main private equity fund. "At first, the investment world seemed like a way to make a lot of money, gain useful skills, and really be in the thick of things," she says. "I had been raised with the idea that success means a big salary because my family had come to America from China without a lot of money. But I have concluded that I need to make just a minimal amount of money to be happy and that it's more important to feel that I can identify with what I'm doing for my career."

She decided that a career devoted to social and environmental issues might just provide the elusive meaning that she and other millennials are seeking. But she didn't abandon the business world for an environmental activist group. Instead, like Mira Inbar, she headed to Berkeley for an M.B.A. degree. After graduation, she took a position in PG&E Corp.'s M.B.A. leadership development program in hopes of working on renewable energy and strategic social responsibility projects for the San Francisco–based utility company. Her path is characteristic of many millennials, who choose to work from within the system. "I like the thought of going to work for a company that has enough financial resources to make a meaningful difference," Cheung says.

To be sure, the millennials aren't candidates for sainthood. Their good intentions are certainly commendable, but they aren't entirely selfless. Some have volunteered for public service projects partly so that they could beef up their resumes to impress college admissions officers and corporate recruiters. "Getting into college is so competitive," says Cheung, "that people do try to differentiate themselves with public service activities on their applications."

Although the millennials may be quite passionate about changing the world, they are hardly the first generation with such ambitions. Indeed, many millennials are the children of activist baby boomers who staged sit-ins and boycotts to protest the Vietnam War, the plight of migrant farm workers, discrimination against women and minorities, and environmental pollution. This may be the generation for Al Gore's *An Inconvenient Truth* documentary about the perils of global warming, but it was the boomers who helped celebrate the first Earth Day in 1970.

Now nearly 40 years later, it is perhaps fitting that activism is moving from the streets to sites on the Internet. Some new charitable endeavors are wisely reaching out to millennials where many of them spend the most time—online. Instead of traditional phone calls and mailings, more activists are using the Internet as a grassroots organizing tool. Cause-oriented Web sites give people ways to communicate with like-minded individuals, volunteer their time, and contribute small sums of money to their favorite charities. For example, DoSomething.org, a networking site for budding young activists, connects them with a host of causes running the gamut from animal welfare and teen homelessness to global poverty and gay rights.

On the popular Facebook social networking site, a start-up called Project Agape has launched the Causes program with the goal of empowering individuals and achieving "equal opportunity activism." Facebook users are encouraged to recruit their network of friends to support their pet cause. By spring 2008, the cancer research campaign had attracted the most members— more than three million—and donations of more than $60,000.

But as millennials grow older and take on more career and family obligations, some skeptics wonder whether they will live up to their professed commitment to make a difference and tackle such global problems as climate change, poverty, and AIDS. "I want to know if their desire to change the world is a passing fad or a core component of this generation," says Cam Marston, founder of the consulting firm Generational Insight. "I think it's too soon to know that."

Already, though, some employers have noticed conflicting behavior among millennials. For instance, Michael Kannisto, global staffing director at contact lens maker Bausch & Lomb Inc., has become a bit cynical about millennials' dedication to the environment. "They claim they are socially conscious and talk a good game about global warming," he says. "But they have a voracious appetite for consumer goods and want to drive cars rather than take the bus. When it's convenient, it seems, they want to save the world."

CHARITY BEGINS—IN COLLEGE

For some millennials, it's college or graduate school that really awakens their social consciences. Segun Olagunju experienced his moment of revelation in his senior year at the University of North Carolina. A course that dealt with "the dark side of globalization really opened my eyes to another side of business beyond making profits," he says. Now Olagunju, who moved with his family from Nigeria to the United States at the age of seven, hopes to return to Africa and work with banks or consultants that support small businesses there. "I know now that I want to help bring about change in Africa," he says. "It was really North Carolina that introduced me to such possibilities with their focus on social responsibility and sustainability. They really preach a lot about public service."

Virtue is clearly in vogue these days at many business schools. Like Olagunju, other students are seeing a surge in courses and programs dealing with such issues as business ethics, social entrepreneurship, and corporate responsibility. In 2007, nearly two-thirds of business schools required students to take a course dedicated to business and society issues, up from one-third in 2001, according to the Aspen Institute. In addition, 35 schools offer a special concentration or major focused on the social and environmental issues facing mainstream, for-profit businesses.

But students say that still isn't enough. Seven out of 10 M.B.A. students believe business schools should place even more emphasis on training socially and environmentally responsible individuals, according to a survey by Net Impact, an international student organization with a focus on social responsibility.

Berkeley's Center for Responsible Business has become one of the most dynamic academic programs. Students can choose from dozens of different classes with social or environmental content. For example, the Strategic Corporate Social Responsibility course requires M.B.A.s to perform consulting projects for clients as diverse as the Detroit Lions football team and sandal maker Birkenstock. They explore such issues as socially responsible investing, human rights, strategic philanthropy, and public-private partnerships. Berkeley students also are managing a fund that invests in companies that are both financially sound and socially responsible.

The Center for Responsible Business has impressed some companies enough to receive their financial backing. McDonald's Corp. and Gap Inc. have awarded scholarships and research fellowships, and Levi Strauss & Co. makes grants to promote teaching and research.

There's also plenty of activity outside of business schools. More liberal arts students, for example, are creating their own majors with a social or environmental emphasis. At Indiana University, about 25% of the students in the Individualized Major Program in the College of Arts and Sciences are focusing on social issues. "I think there is a great deal of untapped idealism among students," says Ray Hedin, director of the program. He is urging more of them to design their majors around such topics as environmental sustainability, ethnic conflict, race, poverty, religion, and civil justice.

Beyond the classroom, some universities are offering students the opportunity to take on philanthropic projects in far-away lands. For her service learning project at Stanford University's Graduate School of Business, Katherine Boas traveled to Thailand and was inspired by the entrepreneurs grappling with the region's severe poverty problem. She and a fellow student returned later to Thailand and developed a very rudimentary business curriculum for rural villagers dubbed the "Barefoot MBA." Simple stories teach basic lessons about saving, investing, cost-benefit analysis, debt, and price competition. For example, in the lesson on investing, one rice grower saves her profit of 500 baht, while another uses part of her income to buy and raise catfish. In the end, she sells the catfish to other villagers and more than doubles her profit.

"Our Barefoot MBA is, I think, a perfect example of students using M.B.A. skills to further social good," says Boas, who took a job with the management consulting firm McKinsey & Co. after graduating from Stanford. "It also helped solidify our own business training."

Some students are choosing colleges at least partly on the basis of community service opportunities. Frances Nguyen was already considering attending Tulane University in New Orleans, but what clinched her decision were the school's new public service requirement and its role in the city's rebirth after Hurricane Katrina. "I knew I wanted to dedicate myself and my time in college to helping others," she says, "and there was nowhere else that offered the research and academic opportunities, as well as the setting in New Orleans to do a lot of good work."

The university, which itself suffered from the hurricane and had to cancel classes for the fall 2005 semester, created a Center for Public Service and began requiring students to participate in service learning courses and philanthropic projects in order to graduate. "Our admissions office now uses public service as a recruitment tool to reach out to prospective students," says Vincent Ilustre, executive director of the center. "Students like the idea of being part of the rebuilding process, not just by rebuilding homes, but by participating in numerous other projects such as neighborhood survey assessments and policy research." According to Ilustre, applications to Tulane are running about 80% higher than they were before Katrina.

Because of her extensive public service work in high school, Nguyen received a community service scholarship from Tulane. A first-generation Vietnamese American who grew up in northern California, Nguyen quickly immersed herself in a variety of projects when she moved to New Orleans. She joined Big Brothers Big Sisters and twice a week mentors an 11-year-old boy named Myles. They do homework, toss around a football, and talk about anything that crosses the boy's mind. She also teaches English to new immigrants for Catholic Charities, works at a children's hospital, and volunteers to paint schools and rebuild homes. It's a hectic life, but she still manages to get her homework done.

"I think that my peers and I are especially drawn to doing community service because we have been raised in a world where there are a lot of problems, but also with the opportunity to change things," Nguyen says. Her ultimate goal is to become a pediatrician and travel the world helping the poor through the humanitarian organization Doctors Without Borders. "Despite what people might say about my blind idealism for doing good, I can make a difference as long as I can change at least one person's life for the better," she says. "A lot of people feel that the only things that make a difference are grand gestures, but I think that small changes eventually build up to something great as well."

THE GREENING OF RECRUITING

With their strong sense of civic duty, some millennials aspire to work for the Peace Corps and Teach for America. Others hope to start their own new ventures with a social or environmental mission.

But most millennials still expect to work for a large corporation. They won't settle for just any employer, however. They intend to join companies committed to social and environmental responsibility, and they want to be given time by their employers to perform community service. Some young people consider a reputation for corporate citizenship so important that they are even willing to accept a lower salary to work for a company they admire.

Nearly 80% of millennials say they prefer to work for a company that cares about making contributions to society, and 64% claim that corporate social and environmental activities would make them feel more loyal to an employer, according to the survey by Cone and Amp Insights. What's more, over half of millennials say they would refuse to join an irresponsible corporation.

Fortunately, this generation will find a growing number of companies in tune with its values. More companies see good deeds as good business these days. They have come to realize that positive reputations for social and environmental responsibility help attract customers, investors, and employees. That's why more businesses are making their corporate citizenship a key part of their recruiting pitch to the millennial generation.

Merrill Lynch & Co., for example, found that college students today are much more inclined than previous generations to ask senior executives about how much they give back to the community. That prompted the company to add messages about "investing in a greener future" and "helping those in need" to its recruiting brochures. Similarly, Wachovia Corp. recruiters make it a point to tell students about the financial services company's "green building" projects to reduce energy and water consumption.

General Electric Co. recruiters were pleased to find that the company's "ecoimagination" program to develop environmentally friendly products and technologies resonates strongly with millennials. Seth Dunn recruits millennials who are enthusiastic about developing renewable forms of energy, and he sees "an explosion of interest" in his company. "I attribute this largely to ecoimagination, which attracts millennials who want to work for a company that makes sustainability central to business strategy and does not ghettoize social and environmental issues to roles that consist mainly of PR, community service, and donations," he says. "It's a business strategy grounded in the critical sustainability issues that one could argue have been largely left to their generation to solve."

A growing number of companies also are starting programs to give millennials an opportunity to demonstrate their generosity. Timberland Inc., for example, has long been in sync with the millennial generation's priorities. Back in 1992, it began offering employees 16 hours of paid leave a year to do charitable work. The 16 hours gradually expanded to 40, and the boot and clothing maker also started allowing employees to take six-month sabbaticals to work with nonprofit organizations.

Now more companies are following Timberland's lead in their efforts to attract millennials. As part of their summer internships with FedEx Corp., for instance, college students take on community service projects in Memphis, Tennessee, such as fixing up dilapidated apartment buildings, sending care packages to Army soldiers, and tie-dying shirts for patients at St. Jude Children's Research Hospital.

Boston Consulting Group Inc. has created the Social Impact Fellowship Program, which lets incoming consultants work for a nonprofit organization for up to 10 weeks. Some fellows have joined Habitat for Humanity to build homes in such countries as El Salvador, Romania, India, and Mongolia. Others have applied their consulting talent to help nonprofits finance new ventures, develop growth strategies, and improve their operations. Junior consultants also are coaching undergraduate and M.B.A. students on projects for nonprofit groups. "We recognize that students care more than ever before about our firm's commitment to being a responsible corporate citizen," says Carly Janson, director of social impact for Boston Consulting.

Ernst & Young, which has even made corporate social responsibility part of annual performance reviews, encourages employees to volunteer to support both education and entrepreneurship. The accounting firm also selects some of its experienced high performers for three-month service sabbaticals to assist entrepreneurs in Latin America. "The millennial generation thinks we messed up and really wants to improve the world," says Deborah Holmes, director of corporate social responsibility. "We get a staggering number of resumes when we have a job opening involving social responsibility."

In a 2007 study on volunteering, Deloitte & Touche found that nearly two-thirds of 18- to 26-year-olds would prefer to work for companies where they could contribute their talents to nonprofit organizations. But only 39% said their current employers provide volunteer opportunities, and only about a quarter said recruiters even mentioned their company's community service efforts during the hiring process.

"Companies that encourage their people to contribute knowledge and experience to nonprofits will make a difference by giving back to the community and, at the same time, build the skills and morale of their people," says James Quigley, CEO of Deloitte Touche Tohmatsu. Among the accounting firm's volunteer efforts is its annual Impact Day, when as many as three-quarters of its employees set aside their work and make nonprofit agencies their clients.

TIME TO TEACH

To attract millennials, some companies are giving them the best of both worlds. They are partnering with Teach for America, letting new recruits go off and teach for a couple of years in poor communities before starting their jobs. Some employers even pay signing bonuses in advance, before the teaching assignment begins.

Companies had noticed the millennial generation's growing interest in Teach for America and feared they would lose some of their prime prospects to the program. In 2008, Teach for America attracted nearly 25,000 applicants and placed more than 3,700 new teachers in classrooms across the United States, the most ever in its 18-year history.

"Companies saw that they weren't just competing with other corporations for talent; they were increasingly competing with us as well, for students with good grade-point averages and leadership positions on campus," says Matt Kramer of Teach for America. "Now more of them are starting to realize that there's no need to recruit against us. They can recruit the same people we are, but give them two years to develop their leadership skills and have a significant community service experience in the classroom before coming on board."

Starting with J.P. Morgan Chase & Co. in 2006, the partnership program has grown to include some of the major campus recruiters, especially in the financial services and management consulting fields. Among the partners: Citigroup Inc., Goldman Sachs Group Inc., McKinsey, General Electric, and Bain & Co.

Google Inc. also has become a partner, giving two-year deferrals to millennials accepted by Teach for America. During their classroom experience, they are paired with a Google mentor and given a summer internship at Google between their first and second year in Teach for America. "The two-year deferral is ideal because they're not too long away from the business," says Jordan Bookey, a diversity programs manager at Google. "But it still gives young people time to do a little more exploration before settling into a job."

In addition to the deferrals for its own full-time hires, Google is participating in joint recruiting events with Teach for America and is interested in meeting with its alumni after they have finished their teaching stints. "Teach for America does a good job of picking people who are much like the kind of employees we're looking for—creative go-getters," Bookey says. "We also believe their classroom skills are transferable because in both teaching and working for Google, you need to be self-motivated and able to manage a lot of different things and communicate information to a lot of different people. You also need to bring some humor and lightheartedness to the classroom and the job."

For Daniel Marks, a Princeton University graduate, the Teach for America partnership was one of the major selling points when he considered a career at J.P. Morgan Chase. He plans to join the bank full-time in 2009 after finishing his Teach for America assignment at a public high school in Chicago. He received his signing bonus up front, which "wasn't a deal breaker but was still extremely important to me," he says. "It was another sign that J.P. Morgan is behind me and supportive of my work for Teach for America."

Marks felt inspired by a Teach for America presentation during his summer internship at J.P. Morgan. "I was shocked into action by hearing how terrible some inner-city high schools are and the impact that people my age could have," he says. "It got me thinking of the opportunities and advantages that got me to where I was."

Since he started teaching chemistry and physics at the Chicago high school, Marks has found it stressful and heartbreaking at times. He has been amazed to meet teenagers who read at a first-grade level and take 30 seconds to solve a simple subtraction problem. He is also dismayed to see students harassed by gang members on their way to school and 15-year-old girls who are already pregnant.

"But working with students can be an unbelievable joy, too," Marks says. He recalls the exhilaration he felt when a failing student worked with a classmate to improve his math and critical thinking skills and managed to get the highest test score in class one day. "It's going to be difficult," he says, "to walk away after making all these personal connections with the students and the school."

THE SOCIAL ENTREPRENEUR

Some millennials are combining their penchant for entrepreneurship with their social consciousness. At business schools across the globe, more and more students are enrolling in social entrepreneurship courses and participating in social enterprise competitions. For example, there's the annual student-led Global Social Venture Competition, which awards a grand prize of $25,000 to the business plan with the best blend of economic value and social impact. Begun in 1999 at Berkeley, it has grown to include Columbia Business School, London Business School, Yale School of Management, and the Indian School of Business. So far, the competition has awarded more than $250,000 to emerging social ventures, and nearly a quarter of past entrants are now operating companies. The start-ups range from a solar-powered trash compactor manufacturer to an online microfinance business making tiny loans to Third World entrepreneurs.

Through both for-profit and nonprofit ventures, visionary social entrepreneurs hope to develop cures for poverty, global warming, and the planet's many other ills. Social entrepreneurship received a big boost in 2006, when Muhammad Yunus and Grameen Bank won the Nobel Peace Prize. Yunus began making small personal loans to destitute basket weavers in Bangladesh in the mid-1970s and established the Grameen Bank there in 1983 to try to reduce poverty through microlending.

Afton Vechery may not be competing for a Nobel anytime soon, but she did participate in the first social entrepreneurship business-plan contest at Wake Forest University in Winston-Salem, North Carolina. A high-energy, optimistic undergraduate at Wake Forest, Vechery is trying to raise enough money to make a biodiesel reactor facility that will convert excess grease from the university's dining centers into fuel to run campus machinery. Ultimately, she hopes to go national by devising a plan to install small-scale biodiesel reactors in hundreds of institutions.

"Being a scientist and wanting social change are important, but being an entrepreneur is the only way to make that change," says Vechery, a Presidential Scholar for Entrepreneurship at Wake Forest. "If you understand science yet can articulate it in business terms, you will be able to evoke change more successfully and make money in a meaningful way. For me, it's a win-win situation."

The biodiesel project isn't her first social venture. As a high school freshman in Western Howard County in Maryland, she founded Student Advocates for Environmental Water to test well water for contaminants. She eventually started a business to promote education about well-water safety and to locate contaminated wells. "The long hours alone in the lab weren't the high point of my venture," she says, "but when I found a positive test for *E. coli* and was able to let the owner of the well know that he should get it professionally tested, it really made it all worth it."

Vechery attributes her entrepreneurial talent to her childhood years when instead of watching television she kept busy on obstacle courses and craft projects. Her mother would hang her creations throughout the house. "I was allowed the opportunity to experiment, and this early creative stimulation helped me see things in a different way," she says. "The corporate environment is great for some people, but I feel that I am capable of more. Since I will only live life once, I am going to get the most that I can out of this world and give back even more."

CHAPTER HIGHLIGHTS

- Millennials may turn out to be the most generous generation. Many of them feel a strong commitment to do volunteer work in their local communities and even to take on global challenges, such as climate change, poverty, and AIDS. Some skeptics, however, wonder whether millennials will follow through on their professed desire to make the world a better place.

- Colleges and business schools are sparking some of the millennial generation's altruism and activism. Through courses on social and environmental issues and community service projects, schools are helping millennials see how they can make a difference.

- Recognizing the millennial generation's do-gooder instincts, corporate recruiters are wooing students by touting their companies' environmental and philanthropic programs.

- To satisfy the millennial generation's desire to give back to the community, more companies are giving employees time to do volunteer work and granting public service sabbaticals of up to six months.

- As Teach for America attracts more applicants each year, companies are forming partnerships with the organization rather than competing with it for top college graduates. Employers give new hires a two-year deferral to teach in low-income communities before reporting to their new jobs.

- Some millennials are rejecting the corporate world and starting their own ventures to fulfill both their entrepreneurial and their altruistic aspirations. By establishing new for-profit companies and nonprofit organizations, social entrepreneurs hope to come up with innovative solutions to help reduce poverty, fix some of planet Earth's problems, and deal with other social ills.

About the Author

Ron Alsop, a longtime writer and editor for *The Wall Street Journal*, is the author of the books *The Wall Street Journal Guide to the Top Business Schools* and *The 18 Immutable Laws of Corporate Reputation: Creating, Protecting, and Repairing Your Most Valuable Asset*. He also has served as editor of the *Journal's* Marketplace page and its annual ranking of M.B.A. programs. He is a frequent speaker at conferences on the millennial generation, corporate reputation, and business education. A graduate of Indiana University, he lives in Summit, New Jersey, and can be contacted at www.thetrophykids.com.

Index